AT THE POOL OF WONDER

At the Pool of Wonder

DREAMS & VISIONS OF AN AWAKENING HUMANITY

Marcia S. Lauck & Deborah Koff-Chapin

FOREWORD BY DAVID SPANGLER

BEAR & COMPANY
PUBLISHING
SANTA FE, NEW MEXICO

LIBRARY OF CONGRESS CATALOGING-IN-PUBLICATION DATA

Lauck, Marcia S., 1950-
    At the pool of wonder.

    1. Dreams. 2. Monotype (Engraving), American.
I. Koff-Chapin, Deborah, 1952-   II. Title.
BF1091.L38 1989   135'.3   88-33357

ISBN 0-939680-61-0

Bear & Company
Santa Fe, NM 87504-2860

Design: Hine Editions, San Francisco
Photography: Floyd Lee Color Lab, Seattle
Cover Design: Angela C. Werneke
Editing: Gail Vivino
Printed in the United States of America by Arcata Graphics

9 8 7 6 5 4 3 2 1

"Everywhere at all times, in all cultures and races of which we have record, when the greatest meaning, the highest value of life men called their gods or god, needed renewal and increase through life on earth, it began the process through a dream."

—Sir Laurens van der Post

We dedicate this to the Dream that is waking in our midst.

TABLE OF CONTENTS

ACKNOWLEDGEMENTS

There are many people who have been gateways—who in and of themselves were like doors through which I traveled into the mysterious and wonderful realms of the human psyche. Their lives and their stories have so immeasurably enriched my own that I hardly know where to begin in offering my love and appreciation for all they have meant in my life and the encouragement they so readily provided. My deepest gratitude and love goes to my parents, Betty and Tom Stout, for their unfailing support and for how simply and gracefully they live what they taught me as I grew. To my brothers Tom, Jim and Chuck, for being brothers of my heart—for our deep bond forged in childhood and honored and sustained as adults. To Aunt June who nurtured my song in big and small ways. To all the radiant beings of other realms without whose guidance and partnership none of this would have come to pass. To Carol, who was there to show the way when I stepped through the crack into the other worlds coded within the one we know, and to Jim with whom I came to understand the way of the Dream. To my lifelong friends and companions of the four circles—we've charted much of this territory together and it has been through our communion that these dreams have been born. To Georgia for providing her circle of love and prayer. To Deborah, for a rich and wonderful partnership, for exploring the edges with me, and for those golden moments in which we laughed till we cried. To my daughters, Ellen and Beth, for being the lights and teachers they are and for the dance they have brought to my life. And last, but not least, to my husband, Tom, who has traveled half of my life's road with me, for risking and celebrating our deep union, for his unfailing support, and with whom the miracles born of love are unending.

Namaste,
Marcy

I am so grateful to those who have provided the love, support and inspiration which has helped me follow the vision I have always felt calling. My appreciation goes way beyond the names mentioned here.

Deepest thanks to my parents, Marilyn and Harry Koff, for providing an unbroken foundation of love from which I could go wherever I needed; to my Grandmother, Elizabeth, sisters Susan and Roberta, and the whole family for the strong bonds we share and for their encouragement throughout my life.

Thank you to the teachers and companions along the way, particularly to Joe for being a catalyst in an awakening time, and for the role he played in the moments Touch Drawing was being revealed; to Jerry for so deeply seeing and understanding the whole process, and for being who he is; to Gloria for her heartfelt presence, and to Gail for diving with me into the creative depths. Thank you to Jean Houston and the Dromenon 'family' for providing a vibrant field in which to emerge and blossom; to my dear friend and teacher Elizabeth Cogburn for the many magical times of exploring life lived in the Beauty Way, and for creating a temple in which the creative processes are acknowledged as a way of communion; to Hilda Charleton for helping me to trust my own path, and to Alice and Brother Francis for their sweet healing presence.

Thank you to my husband Ross for his ever-present love, support and partnership; to my daughter Aleah for the new dimension of love and growth she has brought me; to Marcy for being such a clear and beautiful partner while manifesting this book within the context of our full lives; and to the Unseen Ones who have always guided my course.

Deborah

At The Pool Of Wonder has been an interweaving dance of many lives, and for this we are grateful. We especially want to thank Emily Day for being the serendipitous, unsuspecting matchmaker who brought our work together, and Hank Hine, of Hine Incorporated, who, with his skill and sensitivity, worked with us to develop a design which would express the independent development yet common themes of our two bodies of work. David graciously offered to write a foreword for us and has brought his extraordinary perspective and lucidity to the underlying ground of our work. Carolyn lent her love of story and her editorial skills and Joanne provided a heaping measure of enthusiasm, encouragement and support in any number of small and large ways. Our husbands, Ross and Tom, have navigated every step of the book's emergence with us. Ross brought his sensitive eye to the design, his listening to the intrinsic balance and harmony between each dream and image, and his deep affinity for what has been called the "pattern language" in architecture, but which surely speaks of the more universal, unfolding patterns of life. Tom spent many an hour editing the manuscript, moving in and out of the shifting images and scenes of the dreams. Careful never to disrupt or violate their integrity, he enabled the dreams to emerge more precisely with his well-placed questions and the swift strokes of his editor's pencil. That they both gave us the best of their skills, the many uninterrupted blocks of time we needed, and the depth of their love is a gift beyond counting. And lastly, our heartfelt gratitude to Bear and Company for meeting us at the pool of wonder, for their affirmation, and for enabling the dreams and visions to fly.

FOREWORD BY DAVID SPANGLER

Where do we come from? Our bodies, at least, come from the biochemical relationships and pathways that constitute each living cell. We are the children of DNA and RNA, of amino acids and polypeptides. When I think of myself, however, I identify with far more than protein chains and carbohydrate metabolism. I am my hopes, my fears, my dreams, my memories, my visions, my desires. There is an inner me whose body of thought and feeling roams far beyond my continental shelf of skin and bone to explore the deeper seas of communion and imagination beyond.

Similarly, a civilization is the externalization of the dreams and aspirations of its people. It is an inner narrative tangibly written across time in stone and marble, steel and plastic, magnetism and electricity. A civilization may be shaped in part by its environment, but the visions of its citizens wield a sculptor's chisel every bit as strong as earth or sea, wind or rain, forest or dry land.

In short, as individuals and as cultures, we are creatures of two worlds, one of flesh and mineral, the other of thoughts and feelings, dreams and imagination. Both worlds fascinate us, challenge us, allure us, and teach us. From each we learn of who we are. As science and technology continue to uncover and reveal new layers of insight into the outer realm, however, it is the inner world that increasingly beckons us as a new frontier. In its mysteries lie important secrets of our own genealogy, clues to the infinite wonder from which we spring and towards which we are awakening.

As the authors state, this is a book of "dreams and visions." It is an exploration of this inner frontier. It is a visit to a realm that is as much our birthplace as our mother's womb or our world's ecology. The domain of dreams and visions is as much our native land as any piece of earth or sky-raised city upon which or within which we may dwell. It is where we discover and take on the qualities and images that make us human.

In the middle and late Sixties I lived just a few miles south of San Francisco in the town of Redwood City. In those days, Berkeley across the Bay with its anti-war, free-speech rallies and protest and San Francisco with its hippies, Flower Children and psychedelics were like two opposing states of mind. One sought change in the outer world and sought to grasp political power; the other sought change through inner transformation and sought to grasp a new vision of reality. To the tuned-in, dropped-out groupies of the Haight-Ashbury scene, the campus radicals across the Oakland Bay Bridge were filled with sound and fury, perpetuating cycles of violence and oppression by refusing to recognize that real change has to come from within. To the activists, the blissed-out mania of drugs, occultism, psychobabble, and love beads was an escape from the real world, surrender and disempowerment in the face of hard-edged reality. Both groups, however, had more in common than they had differences, for both were offspring of a singularly powerful and shared dream. Though they differed in strategy and tactics, both harbored a common vision that change was possible, that a new world was around the corner, and that civilization could become safer, more humane, more compassionate, and more in harmony with the earth. Though they expressed it differently, both acknowledged the potential of a power within humanity and within the world that could transform history and set us all on the road to a better future.

This power is at the heart of the dream these two approaches shared, and, though they preferred not to recognize it, that was shared as well by the very Establishment they challenged and confronted. This is the dream of an awakening humanity, a humanity becoming ever more aware of its inner and outer nature, ever more sensitive to its connectedness to the rest of creation, ever more attuned to its potentialities and responsibilities. This dream is not the sole province of any one group of people anywhere in space or time. It has been dreamt by our ancestors back into prehistory and it has been dreamt by men and women of all colors and cultures. It is a human dream, a species vision. It is part of what defines us.

This dream is what has built civilizations and it has motivated attempts to escape from or reform civilizations. It has inspired the creation of nuclear-power plants with their seeming promise of unlimited energy to help humanity, and it has inspired the efforts of anti-nuclear proponents to find cleaner, safer ways of meeting our energy needs. It has inspired capitalists and socialists, Christians and non-Christians, mystics and agnostics, thinkers and doers, for there are few who do not want to leave a better world and a better humanity as gifts to their children and grandchildren. In short, the dream belongs to all of us and has uncounted ways of expressing itself.

The dreams of Marcia Lauck and the paintings of Deborah Koff-Chapin are among those ways. It could be argued that these dream tales and visionary artworks are too personal and idiosyncratic to have wide relevance. At times it is as if we have inadvertently opened up someone's private diary, invaded a private mythology, or become spectators to someone else's inner journey. Yet at the same time these dreams and pictures have a fascination, an allurement. Beyond their personal elements, they speak to us in images and colors, symbols and suggestions that bridge into the impersonal, the transpersonal, the co-personal. They may not specifically be our dreams, but they remind us of the dream, the shared dream of an awakening, unfolding humanity.

Our task in reading this book is not to agree with it or disagree with it, to judge the content of the dreams or the style of the artwork. We can do these things, of course, and nothing should be exempt from the proper exercise of the critical eye and the discerning heart. However much we may be moved by Marcia's words or Deborah's art, we must still determine how they fit into our lives and where the point of proper integration and assimilation may be. Still, it is not simply as content but as a reminder that this book has power. Can it remind us of the Great Dream we all share? Can it remind us or inspire us to find that Dream in ourselves, in our own way, in our own words and images? Can it remind us to find ways to live the Dream in our lives, to advance the awakening of humanity through the awakening of our particular embodiment of it?

We are encouraged in this process by the very nature of this book itself. When Marcia recorded her dreams and Deborah painted her visions, they were not consciously collaborating on a book. Without knowing each other, they were each responding to an inner calling and an inner search. It was after they met and shared both the dream record and the paintings that they realized that they had independently touched a common Dream, a shared Vision. Each had given it her own particular shape, but behind this particularity lay the universal, that Great Dream, that collective Pool that we may each touch and from which we may each be empowered and transformed.

It is ironic that the purpose of a dream is to awaken us. A visitor from the unconscious, a dream may challenge us to look beyond the surface of our lives, to look at that inner source of our beingness that shapes us and our world as surely as our DNA shapes our bodies or our architecture shapes our cities. Marcia and Deborah offer their personal experiences with that inner place to inspire us to do the same. Your dreams and mine may be different from theirs, but they can come from the same place and lead us to the same future. They can be seeds for our own further awakening to tap that inner pool of wonder and wisdom that refreshes and renews us all. Of all the things our world needs now to help us and it survive and prosper, the gifts of that pool may well be the most needed and the most life-giving of all.

David Spangler

PREFACE

In July of 1986, during the dark, pre-dawn hours, Deborah Koff-Chapin and I sat sipping tea and sharing the deep symmetry of our visions. Hers was born in 1974 out of her explorations as an artist; mine paralleled hers through twelve years of nightly dream journeys into deep wells of consciousness. Even before we met, we shared a common, fundamental predilection: to find some way to lift the veil between our personal experiences of the world and their source—to live close to the heart of creation.

For Deborah, the union of her work and her vision began as she was cleaning an inked glass sheet in the printshop on her last day of art school. She placed a paper towel over the ink, but before wiping it off, she playfully moved her hands on the rough paper, creating lines on the underside through the pressure of her fingertips. In an ecstatic flow of inspiration, image after image poured directly through her fingertips onto successive paper towels. Though at first childlike and primitive, these images were a direct, immediate expression of each moment as it passed. Underneath the creative dialogue between her hands and the paper there was the intuitive recognition that some profound, life-directing, and affirming revelation was surfacing. She began to take seriously what had been given in play. From that initial experience, through times of pain and soul searching, Deborah turned to the drawing board as her inner mirror. Using this simple but potent process which she named "touch-drawing," her feelings could be tapped, released and transformed. Each drawing became a stepping stone leading her more and more deeply into the universal roots linking self and source.

For me, the decision to explore the world of dreams was the key. I hoped, through this study, to come to a greater understanding of myself and my life. I was unprepared, then, for the nature and scope of what was to unfold from that initial resolve. Over a period of several years, as I became familiar with the inner territory of dreaming, startling changes and accelerations of consciousness began to occur in my life. Each night, I found myself propelled into new dimensions of lucid awareness, and the boundaries between my waking and dreaming selves dissolved. My dreams began to emerge from a central core of indescribably brilliant light whose very essence was a deep and abiding love. Gradually, this light clothed itself in images, visions, and stories, and splashed out into the events of my life and the lives of others. Far from representing personal, subconscious dramas, these dreams had become a rich commentary on the evolution of consciousness.

As Deborah and I explored the inner depths, we found ourselves delving into the potent archetypes which lie at the heart of our humanity and at the heart of creation. Deborah, hands dancing on paper, drawing out subtle impulses from those inner realms, made these primal patterns visible through the mirror of the drawing board. I, through my nightly appointments with the universe, brought them back in symbol and in story.

The story told by the dreaming alone, or by the touch-drawings alone, was record enough of the vision which had been expressing itself through each of us. But for us to sit together that morning in the kitchen and watch dreams and drawings find their counterparts—weaving, as they did, a coherent and stirring whole—was like hearing the distinct voices of a vast, synchronous fugue come together. Dream by drawing, drawing by dream, the unity of the themes resonated and amplified, and, in those early morning hours, *At the Pool of Wonder* emerged.

What we share in these pages seems to be part of a broadening shift in consciousness that is happening around the globe as humanity confronts the many ecological, political, and spiritual challenges which face our world. One by one, in the privacy of our own hearts, many of us are choosing to live our lives in ways that connect us firmly and consciously with those deeper sources which give rise to and renew ourselves and our world. Perhaps, as each of us finds and nourishes those sources of inspiration in our personal lives, we are discovering keys to renewal for our planet as well.

We offer these dreams and images as they emerged into our lives in the hope that they will add to the remembering of who we are, and to the discovery of all that we are called to become.

Deep peace of the shining stars,

Marcia S. Lauck and
Deborah Koff-Chapin

January 1987

ENTERING *At The Pool Of Wonder*

In the following pages, dream and drawing pairs are presented primarily through the chronology of the dreams. It is important to understand that they are not intended to relate a story in the traditional sense. They more closely resemble a mandala whose pattern emerges from their interweaving themes. As such, they are best met from the center of your deepest attention and awareness.

THE TRANSLATORS

As I prepare for sleep, the white orb of a full moon casts a soft radiance through our bedroom windows, creating a silver patch at the foot of the bed. I settle underneath the covers, wondering what the night's dreaming will bring. My thoughts touch lightly back to the evening's events: our community of friends had gathered quietly and purposefully to open ourselves to the turning of the seasons from summer to fall. As has been our custom at such gatherings, we celebrated our deep connectedness with the Earth, and with God, who has woven our lives together with the rhythms of the natural world. The evening's ceremony envelopes me, and then I let it all go as sleep arrives. There is the now-familiar sense of rapid passage away from my known surroundings, and I feel my dreaming self launch into the unknown, drawn to an appointed destination.

I surface after an unknown period of time, sensing into the nature of the space. Underneath and overlaying everything is a brilliant light. I am without body or form, a spark of pure knowingness swimming in a vast omniscient sea. I wait, knowing that the purpose for which I have been called will be revealed when all is ready.

Out of the formless radiance, wavelike bodies of awareness assemble and express themselves in ways that enable me to identify them. This is a great gathering of many expansive, yet familiar, collective consciousnesses: the human race, the nature kingdoms, the animal kingdoms, the living Earth, the full moon, the fiery sun. Then, as if blown by a solar wind or some unknown breath of the Spirit, these consciousnesses converge, rising into a single, towering wave. They crest and break, washing over and through me, infusing my awareness with their very essences. Luminous, multicolored transparencies and images emerge into my awareness, streaming out from this teeming profusion. Undergirding, guiding the flow of these images so that I can understand them, is an unseen, but deeply felt presence.

I watch, spellbound, as Earth's story—all possible patterns and combinations of planetary evolution, past, present, and future—unfolds in images unbound from the linear constraints of time. In a majestic, surging dance, these images interweave, forming shimmering ribbons of color and light which spiral together like some vast double helix of DNA. Each of us, and all of us combined—man, woman, animal, plant, moon, sun—are part of a great cooperative endeavor forming the Earth we know. We are coded within each other's genetic material in ways that make for unceasing communication between us all, if we but learn how to listen to it.

I gasp, as the powerful figure of a shaman suddenly emerges out of the center of the spiral. His eyes catch and hold mine, commanding my attention as the ribbons of light change into the curling smoke of a medicine pipe. Without warning, he transforms into a massive stag, though his eyes remain the same. The Deer Man is a shaman of great knowledge and power. I intuitively sense that the Native American medicine people know him well, but what is startling to me is the strange series of names I call him: "the man from Atalanta . . . Atlantis . . . Atlanta."

As I say these names out loud in the dream, trying to find some shred of familiarity or meaning in their sound, small quakes ripple through me—further ruptures along the fault lines of my consciousness. Inside, I feel myself plunge through a widening crack into a deep subterranean stream of consciousness. Under the Deer Man's penetrating gaze, I am opened to a great flow of information:

Shamans from all times are directing the movement of these spiraling, luminescent images, bringing them forward in response to the great challenges we presently face. These travelers of the inner dimensions are focusing their wisdom, their knowledge of the imperishable truths of existence, and all their skill toward the Earth, creating a constant stream of energy, power, and information to assist us in this time.

As part of their message, I am given insights concerning my relationship to them and the wisdom they bear. These insights concern my work as a type of receiver/transmitter that allows this knowledge to be communicated, and that translates cosmic sound into images and information coherent to the people of Earth. The knowledge communicated through these beings is to assist us in penetrating through the camouflage of the outer universe into the central mysteries at the heart of creation.

A brilliant scene of Deborah appears in the midst of these tidings. She is also translating, but doing so through her touch-drawing. I instinctively know that what she is working to unite with is the inner model from which the outer drawing will be formed. As I watch, a primary image begins pulsing in and out, presenting seemingly endless variations of itself. In a subtle but tangible dance, archetype and artist fuse, and under Deborah's skilled touch, a drawing emerges, echoing the images which spiraled together earlier in the dream. I start momentarily, for the drawing already exists and hangs in her living room.

I waken, feeling stretched across the multidimensional images of the dreaming, trying to orient myself to my body and to the coming day. The energies which opened me to the shamanic stream had their greatest impact in my chest, and as I come to record this three days later, I am still working to balance my body. Each night now, following the dream, I have continued to work with and further expand what was opened, clearing pathways for the wisdom which is seeking entrance.

September 18, 1986

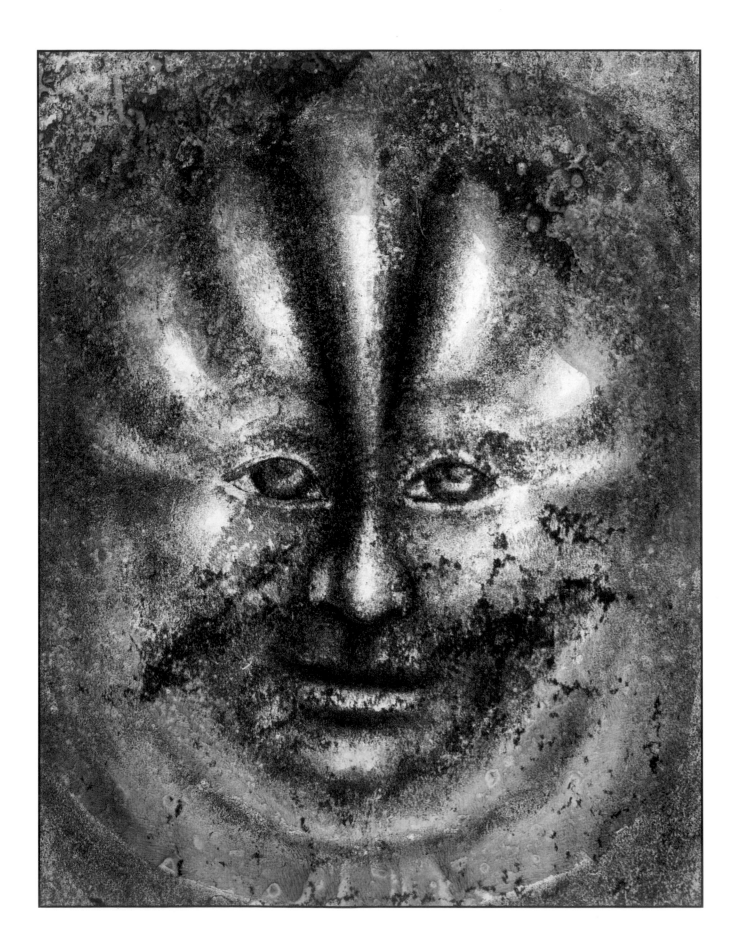

JAGUAR WOMAN

Dreaming opens: I am in a remote, primeval rainforest. Moonlight filters softly down through the dense vegetation and the night air feels cool and moist against my skin. I am sitting in the driver's seat of a car. One level of perception tells me that it is a rusting, gutted shell, abandoned to the jungle. But a slight shift of focus reveals that it is also a fully functional station wagon in which I know I have quite purposefully driven to this appointed place. Without understanding why, I sense it is important to the overall context of the night's work that these two levels merge within me—a synthesis of primal Earth power and modern technology. As I waken further into the dream and begin to locate myself, I recall that I have been waiting here for someone or something.

Suddenly my flesh rises with pinpricks of alarm. Somewhere, from within the hinterlands of the human psyche, an opening is made into the car. I am transfixed, stunned into immobility. Though I am unable to turn around to see with my eyes, an inner screen of vision opens. I watch as the air behind me parts. Stepping through this crack between realities, into the seeming solidity of the back seat, is a wild and powerful jungle cat—a jaguar. Her primal presence bores into my back, and I dare not make even the slightest perceptible movement. She paces restlessly from side to side—her deep, rumbling warning rattling through me; her power tightly coiled, like a snake gathered to strike. Her low growls tell me that I must not turn to approach her. There is a test here: I understand that I am to sit quietly, opening as much as I can into the deep underlying unities of creation. In unshakeable calm, I am to radiate my bond with and love for the Earth, for the Earth's creatures, and for this jaguar in particular. I am to do so in the midst of the imminent threat of her untamed wildness, knowing that either she will choose to come closer or, if my intent is not clear, she will attack and kill me.

After what seems like hours of reaching and sustaining this deep communion, I feel the brush of whiskers against the nape of my neck—a soft gentle caress. Slowly, she steps over the seat that separates us and sits beside me. I become acutely aware of the feel of her coat against my arm—silken, yet bristly . . . my nostrils fill with the pungent scent of her wildness, and my heart nearly bursts with the intense love and bond that has been forged between us. She lifts one of her paws into my field of vision and firmly places it in my lap. Everything heightens now, as if some noiseless sound were crescendoing: I am nearly shaking with the potency of it. As I watch, the paw touching me shimmers and transforms into a woman's hand. In an instant, the transformation is complete. She is no longer a jaguar, but a woman of great power, a shape-changer, dressed in jaguar skins. And though I sense her ability to easily change back to the great cat, she is solidly here with me. We "talk," mind to mind, no words exchanged in the usual sense, and I bring none of our communication back for now, other than the agreement of our meeting. I waken with the skin of the dream wrapped around me, and continue to be stirred deeply by it all day.

May 23, 1980

THE FIREBIRD

I am in a grassy, unpopulated plains area, the scene of many meetings with Native Americans. Everywhere I turn I am flooded with multisensory impressions: the rolling, fragrant prairie, the blue canopy of the sky, the warm touch of the sun on my back. The land speaks to me—not only in a poetic sense, but also literally—speaking its story and its name to my body in a language common to all who inhabit the Earth: human, animal, plant, water, stone. My mind, quiet and uncluttered, listens; my feet touch the Earth, feeling the subtle cryptogrammic pulsing of the land's life rising up into my awareness: this place where I stand has a special purpose. It is named "the birthing ground."

The dream opens further. . . . My personal boundaries dissolve as I become fully immersed in and part of the land's living awareness. It feels like I/we are reaching back into distant, shadowed memories . . . but as my awareness is more wholly merged with the land, the shadowedness lifts and the story becomes clear.

The birthing ground was established when humanity was young. It has been the fertile womb where the new seeds and innovations of each evolutionary stage of humanity's consciousness have been cared for. All possible expressions have been nourished here; all conceivable courses of development have been assessed for their potential to bear the fruit of a species awake to the richness of its divine heritage.

In the images shared, I see that I am working with a man my own age, making sure that all which is presently newborn and potential in this time is properly nurtured. Before long, we walk to an area where I see various eggs and embryos of a great bird—all of which have died or aborted due to improper genetic or environmental conditions. He picks up each one as if it is a museum piece and begins to explain its development and the reasons for its particular failure.

As he speaks, I feel the fluid acceleration of my consciousness, and this portion of the dream becomes a springboard for another more expanded one. In rapid flashes of vision, I plunge into the history of the Plains tribes, but as my inner velocity increases, the images blur and then open out, thrusting me into the rich bed of generativity for all the Indian cultures and the ancient wisdoms by which their societies were shaped. I take in this multileveled view, still hearing my coworker's continuing explanations. I know that the opening of the dream and its emphasis on the "birthing ground" is the entry point for the night's work, but it is clear that whatever is seeking expression needs the full spectrum of the knowledge underlying the Native cultures. It is then that a voice begins to speak through me, overlaying all levels of the dream:

"This bird, whose eggs and embryos you behold here, is an entry point to great power and generativity for the planet. It is known as 'the firebird.' In each age, an attempt is made to bring this symbol of the awakening and initiation of humanity to birth; to unlock its mysteries and to ground them in human experience. All conditions must be met for this to happen: first within the inner recesses of humanity as the embryo develops, and then in the cultural and planetary milieu into which the firebird seeks birth.

"At each new stage of cultural development—as far back as your human storyline reaches—you have sought to bring forth the firebird. What you see here are the attempts, each of which seemingly failed. Yet in truth there was no failure, for with each attempt you gained new knowledge that allowed the building to proceed through the following stages of your culture's development.

"You who seek to embody the sacredness of God's creation in everyday life are, collectively, a womb in which the embryo of a new civilization has taken root. The disciplines you have discerned and practiced, deeming them necessary for the birth of a new vision for humanity, are those which are the genetic building blocks of the firebird. Bridging these awarenesses to your mainstream lives has been your greatest challenge, for without the inclusion of your workplaces, churches, and families, there would be no environment to support the firebird's growth out of the womb. Yet through this communion which you and others of similar purpose sustain, the firebird of a new world will rise on wings of pure light. All the conditions have been met once again, and as you near the fall equinox, *listen:* for the melodic essence of the firebird's return is being sounded once again."

July 3, 1983

SHAPES OF THE FUTURE

I waken into dreaming and find myself staring into the deep red coals of a campfire. The night is so dark that when I look up I can see only the glowing faces of a small circle of companions. Though none are people I've met in my waking life, I realize that I know everyone intimately. My eyes move slowly from one to another, lingering in silent greeting. Each contact is like a window into the depth and breadth of our many-faceted selves, bringing forth our long association and common purposes. It is a warm, familial reunion.

Finally, my gaze comes to rest on one who is a medicine man. So bright is the flare of recognition between us that the others seem to fade away. Then I remember: a long-held vow we had made, which had required our silence and the separation of our once-united work, is to be dissolved tonight. While the others provide a grounding force, the two of us begin a complete merging of our consciousnesses. Inexpressible wonder fills us as our source-selves flow into one another, and our dreams join, spinning in a mandala-like dance of yin and yang. As our deepest selves fuse, the very air starts to vibrate. The scene cracks apart and my mentor appears. I know without asking that she comes with information about the winter festival.

"This festival marks a new beginning for us all," she begins. "A new cycle opens for the Earth. There is an ancient symbol, a gateway to potent energies of transformation, which is to be the womb and the basis of your celebration."

As she speaks, the symbol ◊ shimmers brightly over a scene of the festival gathering. I can see it coming to rest over each person's body as they lie on the floor, eyes closed in a deeply relaxed state.

"This ancient symbol of the Great Mother," she continues, "was adopted by the early Christians, and is called a 'vesica piscis', or 'vessel of the fish'. Its womb-like shape represents the feminine principle of generation. Anyone who allows this sign to merge with their body as they move into sleep will be assisted to come awake in their dreams—to encounter the deeper reality from which they spring. Place yourselves under this sign of the Festival of Identity and open to the dream at the heart of your life. This night will mark a time of expanding awareness for all who participate in the festival's creation and celebration. For, as the Fisher of Humanity said, 'Where two or more are gathered in my name, there I am in the midst of you.' The spirit and seal of the Christ will be moving within and among you this night and all nights, kindling your wakening to all that is to come and to the parts you are to play in God's unfolding plan. Your 'yes' is all that is asked for."

As she finishes speaking and the scene begins to recede, a luminous vesica piscis rises up, enveloping the dream in the Great Womb that gives all things birth in the fullness of time.

October 28, 1983

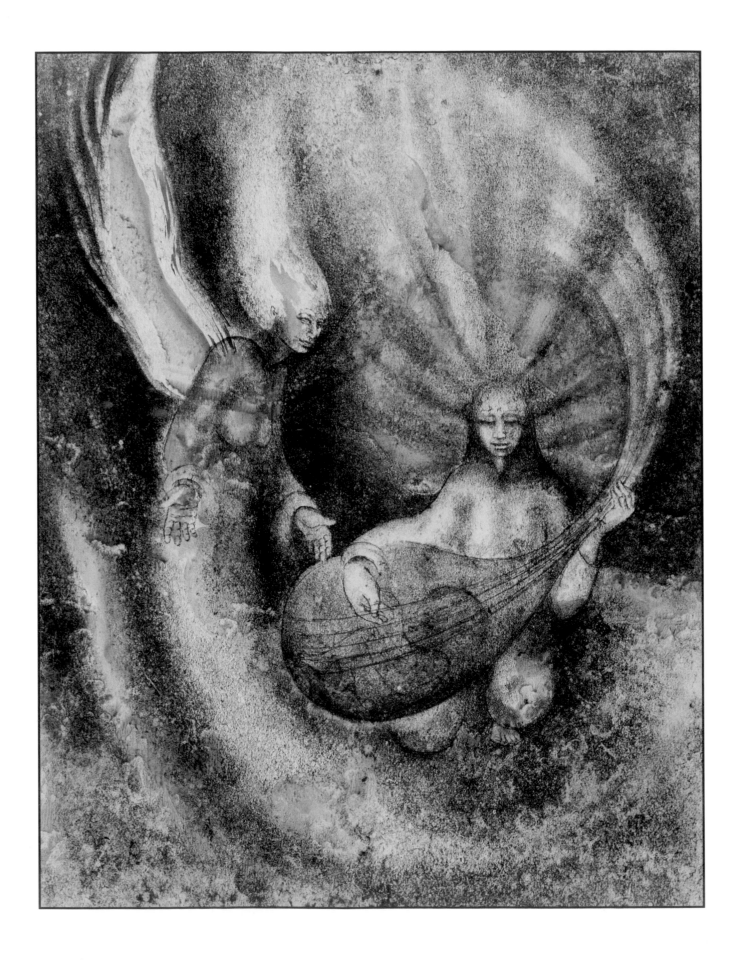

PASSING OF THE OLD

At the close of what feels like a long and involved dream, I am shown a view of Earth from outer space. Like a snake shedding its skin or a chick breaking the confines of its shell, I see the planet shudder and heave, and the surface of the entire globe cracks and breaks. From miles above the planet and then also from close up, I witness the breaking apart of the recognizable order which we who inhabit this Earth have known.

December 10, 1983

. . . AND GOD GREW WINGS

Yesterday's dream has left an almost unbearable heaviness and the sure knowledge that as the Earth shakes off the old familiar topography, similar quakes are occurring within everyone and everything I know. Later this evening, I take time in the quiet dark, seeking a place to rest with the heaviness that accompanies such transitions, and a way to open the door to the deeper purpose of the dream.

The night's dreaming opens and involves aligning and resolving many energies—a clearing after the quake—so that something new can be built, and a new Earth can be formed from the shifting land masses. I waken and nurse the baby around 6:00 A.M. and crawl back into bed, still knowing that nothing has settled. I move back into sleep, and wait within the dark of the dream. This scene opens:

After much searching and with great relief, I locate the room in which I am to sit quietly and open myself to my part in the upcoming winter festival. I open my inner senses fully and discover that this place is the central headquarters of a vast communications network that spans the globe. Somehow, what happens here regarding the winter solstice will be broadcast deep within the racial consciousness of mankind. My guitar is with me, and I understand that I am to begin the alignment of the festival energies by tuning it. As I bring the strings into proper relationship with each other, I am also aware that I am gathering the energies of everyone who will build the festival, tuning us all like an instrument on which the solstice is to be played.

I am sitting at a white work table. In front of me is a large blank sheet of paper. As I meditate, tuning both the guitar and all our consciousnesses, shapes begin to burn their way into the paper. Someone who seems to understand what I am doing walks through at this point, and asks if much has come yet. I point to the paper and show him that what has come so far is the chemical model for the nucleic acid connections of the DNA molecule. I tell him that this means all the pieces for the festival are now present, but that what is to emerge from these building blocks of creation is not yet known.

I move further with the tuning process, and as the last note is pulled into relationship with the others, the imprint that is to overlight this festival of identity, of new emergence, appears full blown:

. . . AND GOD GREW WINGS SO THE SEEDS COULD BE PLANTED

AND A NEW WORLD BE BORN.

As I watch, a bright star—herald of Immanuel, God-with-us—flickers and becomes the olive branch of peace, and the branch brought to Noah as a sign of the new land.

The dove rises, bearing the star to its resting place above the Earth . . . the star and the branch alternately emerge, one from the other, as I watch.

I am so absorbed in this continually reforming imprint, so much a part of it, that it is a long time before I can move back. I know I must see who conceived this sign so I can tell everyone on the night of the festival celebration. I burst out laughing when I see the author's name signed at the bottom right:

"EVERYONE!"

Through our attuning to the vesica piscis, we have opened this door to the spirit and incarnation of the living God-presence within and among ourselves. Through our communion—our common union—we become the wings, we are the seeds, and within us is a new world waiting to be born.

December 11, 1983

THE PAINTING

Journal note: It is now July 27th, six months since I had this dream. For weeks after the dream came, it continued to fire through my body, altering my cellular terrain as surely as earthquakes raise new land masses where once there were none. Over these months, the dream has found ways to make a home for itself, nested within the many layers of my consciousness. Yet I have only been able to walk softly around its edges, knowing I was not to step into its sacred circle and attempt to translate it into words. Now, however, another dream has come, telling me it is time—that I am to reenter the dream and bring what has been woven into the cellular structure of my body out into language. As I approach the task, the ordinary cohesiveness of my body—cell firmly connected to cell—begins to alter. It is as if the binding substance which holds my corporeal self neatly together is thinning, so that the cells are drifting apart, linked only by a fine web of slender strands. All this is happening as I sit here at my desk, hands amazingly solid on the keys of my typewriter. Vast interstellar spaces yawn between the galaxies of cells which form my body, yet they are bridged by these luminous filaments. Then the dream comes, released at last, its electrical impulses coursing over these inner strands and translating into symbols and language:

I am standing in front of what seems to be an eternally existing, time-less library. Inner sensings tell me that this is a place of convergence for the collective wisdom of the planet. Flakes of snow swirling in an icy December wind blow around me, and I peer into the window of the building. I am here, I know, to look for a Christmas card which expresses a vision of the ever-new birth of the Christ. My gaze comes to rest on a display of cards imprinted with masks and medicine shields. Without warning, the dream cracks open and I am hurled through a crack between worlds. The masks and the medicine shields, alive with power, leap and dance around me. Each is a sign and symbol, a distilled essence of a particular Native American tribe. It is a joyful moment, for everything in me knows each one. I am keenly aware of a sense of rising excitement—never do the shields waken unless great moments are at hand! Then the shields themselves give way, becoming the door for the dream seeking entry.

This is a time for a gathering of all the tribes . . . like the great Sun Dances celebrating the sacred hoop of the world. The setting is in a desert that seems to be both in the American Southwest and in the Holy Land of the Middle East. These continue to be the converging themes of the dream: the interweaving of the Native American and the Judeo-Christian heritages. They are portrayed first through the juxtaposition of the two deserts in a time which unites Christmas with this sacred gathering, and second in my own presence as a representative of the Judeo-Christian tradition among these guardians of the land.

It appears to be night, or at least twilight. The stars are in the heavens, and everywhere there is a soft glow illuminating the events, like firelight. Yet as I focus in, I see that this light emanates from within the things and people who are part of the dream. The time frame seems to be present-day, for I notice that the Indians who arrive come in cars, vans, and trucks which are parked in a large circle around the ceremonial grounds. Great long rows of thousands of wooden folding chairs have been set out facing the place where the rites are to take place.

I move to sit down in one of the chairs, but a native woman takes me by the hand and, pointing, begins to lead me toward the ceremonial stage. I look to where she points and am stunned. Where there once seemed to be only earth and sky, there now stand three immense figures, each towering several hundred feet in the air and formed from the yellow rock of these sacred desert mountains. A series of awarenesses strikes me, each more powerful than the last, and the full weight of the dream washes through me. I feel connections being sought within my present understanding. I am first reminded of the Egyptian monuments of the pharaohs which were moved to safety when the Aswan Dam was built a number of years ago. Then I realize that there are three figures here, just as there were in the crucifixion on Calvary. The central stone giant is a great chieftain arrayed in ceremonial headdress; the other two are not as prominent somehow, again paralleling the Biblical account.

The dream unfolds further. I begin to recollect the days of preparation for this gathering: the cleansing and clearing of ground and participants, the inner alignments necessary to give birth to what is a sacrament of the mysteries. Some tribesmen are working on the construction of a scaffolding on the front face of the statues, and everywhere I look in what is now the bright light of the noonday sun, people are busy, preparing for the ceremony.

It begins to dawn on me that I, too, have a part to play. Other dreams of the past several years, in which I was called and admitted into the sacred seal of this ancient society, cluster around me. Again the dream tumbles and spins like a kaleidoscope, and I begin to draw into awareness the nature of the present event. This is an ancient painting ceremony, performed for time beyond reckoning by these guardians of the sacred Earth. I have glimpses into past celebrations now, and am awestruck. In the process of the painting, these stone giants come alive, glowing with rainbow colors. Through this ceremony they become pathways for power—transcendent carriers anchored in the heavens like the aurora borealis as well as being rooted in the Earth itself. Words elude me. I can hardly touch the power of this event with them.

That I am to somehow participate in the painting is clear now, and I walk with my guide to the base of the mountain out of which the figures are carved. There is an entryway tunneled near the feet of the figures, and we stop before entering to remove our shoes. I am unprepared for the power that hits me when we enter the central statue. I stagger under its impact, and grope for the earthen wall to steady myself . . . my heart is racing and I am trembling—never have I endured such power before. What manner of rite is this? I use the spiral stairs before me, one step at a time, to focus my attention and to still myself. This isn't even the ceremony itself, I think . . . only a time to familiarize myself with the route and the elements of the sacrament.

We reach the top of the stairs, and through another doorway, I can see the gathering's preparations far below. I realize then that we have climbed up through the inside of the center statue, and are now somewhere near the heart/throat/head area . . . how to describe this? . . . snatches of memory come. My work is to involve the painting of the central figure. Somehow in the time of the sacrament and my climb up the spiral stairs, I will fuse with and be transformed into an incarnation of the Great Mother. There will also be a medicine man who will be the earthly counterpart of the Great Chieftain. Everything feels so entwined, so complex here, because I am continually pulled in and out of the two perspectives as I perceive the process of the fusion: myself as a very earthly, flesh-and-blood woman, and myself as the primal archetype of the womb and nurturer who brings all life to birth.

I struggle to get the doors of my perception wide enough. This drama to be enacted is an ancient one that has been played out in every culture since humanity linked its story with Earth's. It has been at the heart of our religions, often, as in Christianity with the crucifixion of Jesus of Nazareth, to demonstrate life's triumph over death and the eternal nature of the soul. These are times when great power is invoked and anchored—power which initiates a new expansion of consciousness and through which humanity signals its readiness to assume the responsibility for a new revelation by calling forth and enacting this greatest of mysteries. This is the process by which the ancient archetypal images at the heart of earthly incarnation are awakened—through whom the great divine energies can be released to quicken all earthly consciousness.

The enormity of what is required here staggers me. I am remembering other times when I have played this same part in the drama. As the time of the ritual approaches, the medicine man takes his seat inside and his body is bound to the figure. The woman takes her place on the scaffolding erected for the painting. I recall then that the act of painting is far more than an external design; every time fingers are dipped in the earthen paints and applied to the stone, it is as if the flesh of the man is pierced with huge quills or needles, stitching power into his body, and into the stone of the Earth. I know that, in times past, all men who have been called to ground the power of this rite have died. Another shock wave hits me then . . . for I remember that, as the fierceness of the pain intensifies as the power enters the man's flesh, it has become part of the rite that he sustain the pain by taking the painter's body in his teeth. In the agony of the transcendence, flesh of man and woman are torn asunder. The shock of this sets me trembling again. I remember large chunks being torn away from my right breast in other such rites, and that I, too, have died.

Now, as this ceremony prepares to open, I surrender my life once more, knowing that in the past it was through the ceremony's release of these energies to the evolving consciousness of humanity that I found my life and my purpose. This is the part I am to continue to play—to serve the waking of the Earth, transcending my present form to release the energies that come through this rite. But wait—the Earth rocks beneath me, and a new awareness tears through my body: *this time will be different.* It is again clear that humanity will take new steps to greet its divinity, its part in the cosmic drama, yet I know that for the first time in this ritual's enactment, neither the man nor I will die. What changes everything is that I am a nursing mother.

With this realization, I am catapulted into the actual rite itself . . . the milk is pouring out of my body, nourishing, healing the man as the painting proceeds. This milk, so basic to human life, will allow us passage, without the necessity to reenact the crucifixion and resurrection once again. I am reminded of a woman pastor telling about the original Hebrew translation of a particular Biblical passage in which Jesus is referred to as a nursing mother. Later translations altered this reference to his being the "waters of life."

The celebration explodes into my awareness—the stone giants, alive with light and power, a rainbow bridge between heaven and earth, northern lights in the sky, towering mountainous archetypes rooted in the Earth. Joy sings through me—through my temporal roots. We can do it! We will bring a consciousness of all that is sacred to birth without destroying the Earth we know.

As I return to my body, time warps back into its familiar contours and the dream simultaneously coils back into itself and into the womb of time. The drama has not yet emerged in our time. Through its subtle movement in my body, I feel the story moving to intersect with the here and now. In the moment before I waken, the dream and time align. The many spinning images snap into a single frame: everyone is in their right place. I see myself entering the base of the statue. I reenter my body, knowing that the preparations are complete and the ceremony is ready to begin.

January 28, 1984

SIGN OF THE TOTEM

A long night of dreaming. I waken after ten hours of sleep in the same position I started in. Much of the dream I am not able to bring back, but what I waken with is potent and vivid:

I am standing on what appears to be an enormous natural bridge. My eye scans the sweeping arch, noting that, rather than spanning oceans or bodies of water, this bridge soars upward, vaulting into seemingly endless dimensions, fording layers of increasingly expanding consciousness. One end is Earth-anchored, the other stretches into unknown realities. I wait, poised in a precise inward balance . . . listening. I know only that I have been summoned here to be given a sign, for divine ordinance to reveal its will in the pattern of my life. When I feel the familiar inner pull which signals the dream's readiness to open further, I release into it, and find myself pivoting towards Earth. A rush of pure, unalloyed happiness floods through me as I take in the depth and breadth of our world's natural beauty. In sheer joy, I feel myself lifted off the bridge and carried aloft by those inner currents. My body gathers momentum and I am sent streaming earthward, plunging—not into water—but into the land itself, dissolving into the womb and marrow of the Earth.

After a time, I find myself back in my body, on the bridge. I suddenly become aware that another presence has joined me, and even before I turn to see who or what it is, I feel the relentless pressure of its intent bearing down on my psyche. I turn to see an ancient totem moving towards me. Its power is stunning. I can't remember ever seeing anything like this. Not only is it painted in what I intuitively know is a Native American design, it is also *alive!* In the exact instant that I understand that this aboriginal deity is a lion, it springs toward me with a deafening roar. An inexorable force compels me to meet it. I, too, leap,

49

opening myself to its power. As we collide in midair, I hear an explosion of sound, and we are spun dizzyingly into some far-away vastness.

When my feet meet solid ground, I find myself standing next to the medicine man who has been so much a part of my dreaming these past years. I understand he has brought the totem to life, and that through the lion's power we have leaped through the worlds into an ancient, lightless cave. I send out feelers, tendrils of awareness, sensing into every nuance, every vibration which emanates within this underground lodge. Gradually my vision clears and the cave becomes filled with light. Some sort of cryptic message is chiseled into and covers the smooth, rock walls, like the hieroglyphs found in Egyptian tombs. Impulse tells me that we are to place our hands on these precisely tooled symbols. Together we approach the walls, astonished to discover that these stone symbols are alive. They begin to impress themselves into our awareness, transmitting their information through patterns of vibration which are directly assimilated into our genetic coding. The material is so vast that I can barely grasp its overall scope with my mind . . . the rest coils itself into my cells and will find its way into my dreams in time. . . .

This is an ancient Earth-teaching which was transmitted in the early years of the human race. Through the skills of shamans, this teaching emerged into many different tribal cultures as the painting ceremony, and despite the relative geographic and cultural isolation of those early communities, their ceremonies bore a marked similarity to one another. These potent rituals, in which a body or a tribe was painted with earth pigments, became a way for the ageless wisdom and regenerative power of Earth to be wakened within a human being . . .

Somehow, as I hear this, my body is undergoing the process of being painted. These rituals harnessed incredible power that nothing in Western society has even remotely tapped . . . all modern medicine as it is practiced today is but a pale shadow of the enormous energy that was— and still is—able to be released for healing and empowerment through these ancient ceremonies and rites. I am unable to translate more into words yet, but know that I am now involved in the reclamation of this knowledge and that I am to work with its activation and use at this time in our planet's life.

When our bodies have fully absorbed the cave's teaching, the medicine man and I find ourselves once again on the bridge. We are deep in conversation, walking back toward the Earth-end where my husband waits in our car for me.

"I can't even say I'm frustrated or impatient for the next sign," I say, "Because I know everything unfolds in only the most perfect of times. All I know to do is wait until the sign comes."

"That is what I'm here to tell you," he says earnestly. "*This* is the time—the sign has come through the totem. I *know* it. I dreamed it. I dreamed *you* this night!"

With these words, we reach the end of the bridge. He takes my shoulders in his hands, our eyes meet, and I waken.

April 24, 1984

CALLING THE GODDESS HOME

I waken on this Mother's Day morning with a most powerful dream. It is another of those great archetypal dramas like the painting ceremony dream of last year, in which the personal and universal are so seamlessly blended.

I waken into vistas of great radiance . . . I know and am known . . . without form . . . in unbroken communion with the Light that gives us birth . . . unspeakable joy, celebration without end . . . all interwoven with what must be the music of the spheres. . . .

And then the glory distills: I feel myself condense into sunlight, air, water, and in a final flash of light become a woman hovering over a vast primeval sea, like Botticelli's Venus being born from the ocean, standing naked on a shell.

I seem to split into two women here—one who feels like my present self, and an ancient archetype of the eternal feminine. There is a sense of dancing, sailing, bodies so diaphanous that there is no separation between elements and selves. We become aware of a gathering darkness, and the climate changes from one of brilliance and buoyancy to a heavy brooding. Our shapes become more solid with the gathering storm clouds, the chilling winds, and the rising waves. It seems as if our bodies are becoming denser in response to creation's magnetic pull, and there is a moment when I am again fully myself as I am plunged into the icy spray. Yet the bleedthroughs continue with this other half, the Goddess. We become separated by the climbing waves, and I see alternately through her eyes and then my own. The vortex of this primal sea shapes the Earth and its land masses . . . and then I am carried further into incarnation, still connected by an umbilical cord of consciousness with the Goddess.

Now I am fully myself, on land, calling up the peoples of the Earth to rescue the woman lost at sea. There is one sequence that stands apart and is heightened here:

I am meeting with the ancient yet ageless black woman who has appeared as the tribal storyteller and genealogist of humanity in other dreams. From her vast store of knowledge, she tells me the name of the one whom we seek, but it is clear that this is only one of a whole litany of names that belong to her. In my mind the tribal woman projects an image of names written on paper . . . next to the number seven is the name Wu Wei. I search inside for the meaning of this, and then recall Dolores LaChapelle having written about the Taoist concept of wu wei, meaning "refraining from activity contrary to Nature or the whole. . . . The roots of this went back to the matrilineal cultures based on the ancient Chinese creation-goddess myths . . . 'wu wei' was letting things work out their destinies in accordance with their intrinsic principles."[1]

Then I am with a man—the two of us will be the ones to risk the now-raging seas. I check to make sure he is prepared to sustain himself in the turbulence and the depths to which we must travel, and then we dive into the waves together. Again, my identity splits or seems to, for I both enter the water, and somehow rise far above it at the same time. My consciousness focuses primarily in the identity above the stormy sea, and I begin to sing a powerful song, summoning the peoples of the Earth to join with me in calling the Goddess home.

A vast circle of men, women, and children gather on the shore below the promontory where I stand, and I guide their voices in the ancient patterns and melodies. We sing, voices gathering strength and power, and out of the ocean rises a company of beings of light—angel-like. In the midst of them is an enormous shell-like egg tinged with the pink of the sunrise. I know it contains that which was lost, and all that we now seek to restore the harmony to our world. The shell is not yet open, though I know that it comes out of the depths in answer to our call. When it does open, it will release its knowledge and food for the world to reclaim. We all leap in the air, and a cry of joy fills my ears as the dream closes and I waken.

May 12, 1985

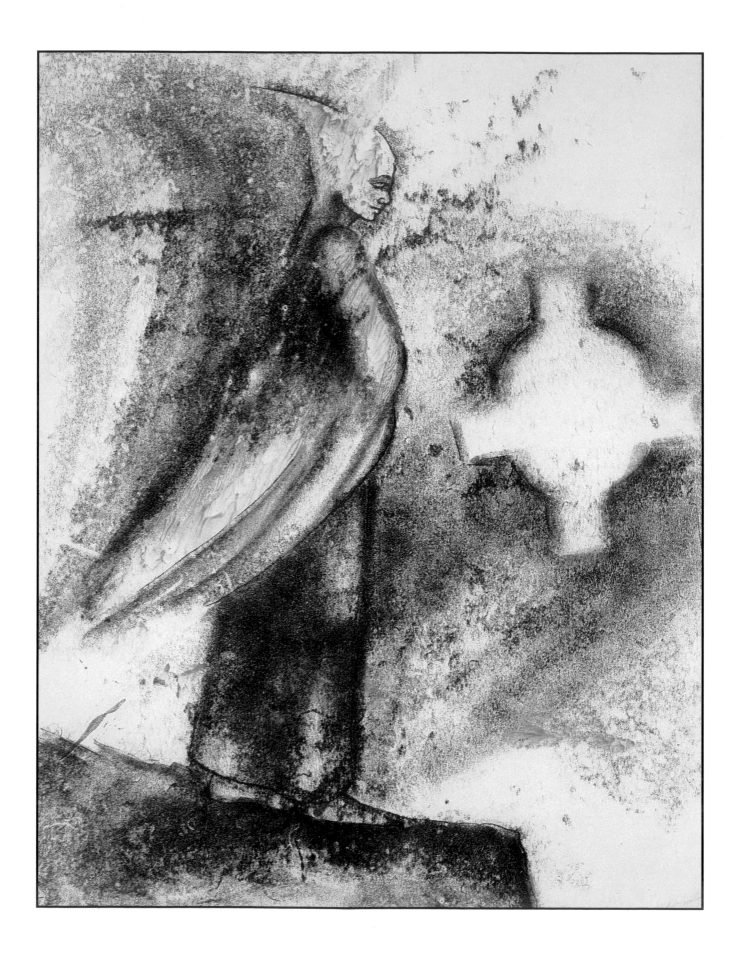

SACRED ISLAND

Dreaming opens: I am not in body, but seem to be scanning the Earth, as one might scan a rapidly spinning globe, from a point in far distant space. Land masses and bodies of water flash by, and I wait for the location that will align with the inner coordinates I hold as part of the night's work. Suddenly I feel the placement deep within my awareness. It seems that the world's spinning slows as I am pulled closer, and I let the planet go around once more in its axial spin until the magnetic attraction between the planet and my own essence intensifies. I gather my dream body around me and let the pull carry me into the physical environment of the Earth.

I find myself over the ocean, being drawn toward an island. My thought is that this island is somewhere off the coast of North America, but as I open to it further, I realize that it is the distinctly white Anglo-Saxon feeling of this place I am responding to. I see it first in the full midday sun, and am struck by how intimately familiar it seems.

As I step onto its shore, I also step through a crack between worlds. Time becomes fluid, blurred, and I begin perceiving this place as it has been through many different ages—a virgin clearing, a stone circle place of worship, a stone sanctuary. Underneath the shifting visions, I remain keenly aware of my deep bond with this land. In a flash of insight, everything clicks into place: this is the island of Iona off the coast of Great Britain. With this information, the time frame of the dream settles, and the night's work becomes clear.

There is a thin, gleaming, crescent moon overhead and the air is scented with the sea. I am with a small body of robed people. There are several men holding up flickering, smoking torches and I observe, with some curiosity, that I am the only woman present. I peer through the haze and the leaping shadows, noting that we are in a courtyard surrounded by a stone abbey or monastery. There is power here. I feel it pressing in against my skin, letting me know by its touch that this is the heart of an ancient power point.

The historical period places us in the Dark Ages. I am standing with two men. The one whom I know is the steward of this place in these dark years, and with whom I am deeply connected, is dressed in a simple black cassock with a silver cross around his neck. Some memory stirs within me, and I recall that his name, Columba, means "dove," a name also given to me in a dream many years ago. Wordless recognition passes between us. The other man, like me, has been called from another time. He is in sharp contrast to Columba and me—dressed in showy vestments, rather like a pope. It is obvious that he is a high-ranking official in the church and presides over a cathedral on the mainland, which I believe to be Glastonbury. He comes from the Middle Ages, and it is clear that he is disoriented by this dreamwork.

I listen to the intent of our meeting, and again the times get blurry. I am not certain whether we are interring something of great potency in the Earth or exhuming it . . . in the rapid flashbacks I see that both have occurred in other times, depending on the need of the planet. When the spinning of time stops, it is clear that tonight we are to bring concentrated power out from within the Earth. As we move to do so, the pope-ish fellow starts to object to my—a woman's—participation in so sacred an event, but Columba tells him, in a voice that will brook no argument, that I am essential to what is to take place. I notice, then, that I hold what I think to be a two-headed ceremonial axe in my hands—not sure what it is to be used for, but clear that it is related to the task.

At the moment when the exhumation begins, I am propelled into another time connected to my present life. As this happens, I am aware that only one portion of my consciousness comes back . . . another is still on the island involved in the work. As I am lifted up out of the torchlight, a voice is ringing in my ears:

"This place is hallowed ground. Since the Earth's beginnings, it has been wholly devoted to worship as a place where the developing consciousness of humanity could have a direct connection to the divine vision for itself and the Earth. Much power has been stored here, and for many years it has been unactivated. Because these energies were to remain untapped until a certain stage of planetary readiness was reached, no one with inner knowledge was called to waken them. The need is present now in your time . . . that is why you have been called here." Part of me wonders at the other priest's role, and I hear that he stewards the power point at Glastonbury and has seen to the building of a cathedral over the spot to protect, as well as appropriately channel, those energies. The two points of Iona and Glastonbury form part of the trinity of points required for this night's work.

Then I find myself in my childhood home, anchoring energy, body, and this night's work in the Pennsylvania earth. A man about my own age, who is also involved in the re-awakening of these sacred energies, is standing with me and another woman in the kitchen. I am speaking to him as I pack a lunch to fortify them for their part in all this. One of the items that has gone into the basket is carrot sticks, cut from the mandala of carrots which I spread out like the rays of the sun deep within the womb of the Earth in a dream several years ago. These are a powerful food given to assist him in opening to the work ahead. As I close up the basket, I tell him that he can get a map of the island from friends in our circle that will show the exact location of the power point. Then I look at him with a twinkle in my eye and say, "But knowing you, you won't need a map!" Our eyes meet and we all laugh as they head out the door and for Iona.

Journal note: When the image of the axe came in the dream, I could find nothing about it in any reference books. Ten months later, I was startled to find a book cover bearing this same two-headed ceremonial axe. I skipped through the pages until I found a description of the cover art. Further research in *The Women's Encyclopedia of Myths and Secrets* revealed that the axe, called a labrys, was wielded as a scepter by the ancient Amazonian Goddess under her various names of Gaea, Rhea, Demeter, or Artemis.[2]

October 28, 1985

ALIGNMENTS FOR THE NEW YEAR

This night's dreamwork opens in a series of space warps. I am working intensely with many different groups of people, preparing everyone, it seems, for the coming year's work. Each time I complete the alignments with one group and step through the waiting door to work with the next, I find myself putting a foot down 3,000 miles away or on the other side of the globe.

Each warp in space is accompanied by an expansion of consciousness, and at last I am standing on the summit of a desert mountain, part of a large gathering of people who have come from all the corners of the land. We have been called here, I know, united in our yearning to give flesh to the vision of a world-made-whole, to restore the sacred Earth.

I cry out something in an unfamiliar tongue and everyone responds, forming a living spiral of people which will uncurl itself, snakelike, as we move down the mountain. I raise my arms in invocation, asking for blessings for the tasks ahead, and then begin the procession's movement. I set the rhythms for our descent—a dancing, stamping pattern, and clouds of dust rise from our feet, announcing, even from a distance, that we are on our way. When I reach the plain, I look back over my shoulder and am heartened by the view of all who are dancing this dance, knowing that our lives and the lives of our children's children depend on it. The woman immediately behind me is watching my feet closely, following my movements. I start to speak to her about the significance of dance, and then become aware that my words are being spoken into everyone's minds and bodies through these patterns of movement.

"You know," I say, "I used to be so painfully aware of how much we were abusing the Earth, and as I'd walk along I would pour what love and healing and light I could into the ground. I knew that just as the body was the soul facing the seasons, so the Earth, too, was alive and 'afire with heaven'. What I hadn't yet fully grasped was the power and wisdom of this magnificent being. What happened as I thought I was helping to heal the Earth was that my love for it became a bridge, and every time my feet or my hands touched the Earth, this being poured power into and quickened *me!* Inside, outside, all around the great wheel, I began to open to the story of the Earth. It taught me about the cosmic drama of creation and evolution, and as I danced the world open, it opened me."

As I finish speaking, I feel our collective consciousness shift, and a doorway appears again. Entering, I find us in the midst of a kind of modern-day trading post. I wonder if there are any quartz crystals for healing, and then laugh as I see row after row of quartz battery watches. We have become a culture surrounded by the power and resonance of crystals and don't even know it!

Then the vibrations of the crystals fuse with us and we are carried deeper into some unknown fastness. All around is the dark, and my every sense is alert, penetrating the unknown. Awareness opens: this is a sacred cave, womb of the Goddess, place of worship. We are here, awaiting the solstice, awaiting the expected but always startling shaft of light from the rising sun as it breaks into the darkness and spotlights the far wall of the cave. In the most affirming and awesome of moments, the cave fills with light as the new year's sun appears. All our eyes are fixed on the spot the sun will strike, expecting to see the ancient spiral illumined. We are stunned then, earthen floor rocking beneath our feet, to see the shadow of the plumed serpent, the feathered snake, cast on the wall. A woman gasps and cries out, "Marcy! Did you see that! It's Quetzalcoatl!"

The shock of the vision sends me catapulting back to my body, and I waken with a start, Quetzalcoatl's name on my lips.

Journal Note: Quetzalcoatl's appearance in this dream was mystifying to me. When no research turned up anything which would unlock the central mystery of the dream, I just typed it up and set it aside. Then, nearly a month later, on the solstice itself, I stumbled on these paragraphs in a book called *Earth Festivals*, and the dream fell into place at last.

"There is an ancient Indian legend concerning Venus, the Morning Star, and the period of nine hells, which began, in the words of Tony Shearer, when 'we became more involved with our own creations rather than with our earth mother and her gifts.'[3] This beginning of the first hell coincided with the year Cortez landed in Mexico. The last, the ninth, will end in 1987. Toward the end of the the ninth hell there will occur a great longing for unity—for wholeness. The return of the Lord of the Morning Star, Quetzalcoatl, will herald deliverance from the ninth hell.

"From South America to the Great Plains in our own country and from the time of the Toltecs down to the present, the Morning Star has continued as a central symbol in Indian thought. This mysterious star, which appears and disappears, brilliantly suspended between night and day, symbolizes the union of opposites—day and night, right and left, conscious and unconscious—holding all in balance.

"Venturing out into space, seeking to learn the secrets of the stars, man saw his first earthrise and the uniqueness of life on this blue-green globe rose into his consciousness. Earth is beginning to acquire a sacred dimension. Astrophysicist Carl Sagan reminds us that way out in space, from Mars, EARTH is the Morning Star."[4]

November 29, 1985

EARTHSEEDS

I move into sleep, feeling as if a powerful, laser-like beam of light is burning a hole in my solar plexus.

Dreaming opens: At first I am again above an island, as in the *Sacred Island* dream of October, but this time it is an island in the Pacific Northwest, not Iona. I am pulled to this place for some unknown reason, and when I settle on the land to wait, I find myself cradled in a stone hollow on a rocky ledge overlooking Puget Sound. My two-year-old daughter is nestled in my lap, and we are quiet and deeply contented. I feel all the activity of the past few days fall away and some deep inner yearning for the land, for vistas of natural beauty, satisfied.

Dreaming splits: on another level I am approaching an ancient stone tower. I open inner perception of this place. Though the tower has the same view of Puget Sound as the other level of the dream, a magic spell, or some sort of binding power has rendered it invisible to all but those who know how to penetrate the enchantment. I stride purposefully through its door and up the narrow winding stairs. There are two people in the working chamber—an older, white-haired woman and her assistant, a balding, bespectacled man in his forties or fifties. They are startled to see me, for no one has broken the binding of the spell for many years. They think my arrival is a mistake, for I watch them check their ley lines of concealment and wait patiently while they try the spells on me which they use on the islanders to keep them away from the tower. When none of these measures yields results, they look to me with interest. I watch their thoughts. . . . Somehow, if I understand and am not bound by their magic, I must have some purpose for being here! It is then that I feel their permission to speak.

"I am here," I say, "because we are to call in some weather for the island: snow! The land must be blanketed, the atmosphere cleared, and the islanders' rhythms slowed down nearly to a standstill for an incoming star-message." As I speak, vivid childhood memories wash over me —newly-fallen snow, air so icy clear each breath ached in my chest—this is the atmospheric purity that we are to call in.

The three of us merge consciousness with the land: tapping deep into Earth, then high into sky, then gathering in all the energies of those who live here. Finally, when the balance of Earth, sky, mortals, and Spirit is in harmony, we cry out, "Let it snow! Let it snow! Let it snow!" The sky fills with big soft flakes. Then I am pulled out of this level of the dream, and as it recedes from me I can see that, already, the ground is white and waiting.

I find myself back on the ledge with my daughter, Beth. I am aware, in some indefinable way, that our bodies and spirits have been fed— deeply nourished, as mother nourishes child—by the unseen but every-where-present spirit of the land itself. Four waterfowl fly into the center of our vision. Through the deep maternal bond with the land comes guid-ance: "Pay attention! Focus your awareness precisely in this moment!"

There is a jolt that shudders up my spine. As the power rises, all the hair on my body crackles and lifts with this lightning-like charge. The four birds flutter down to the water and form a pattern, each of them freezing at one of the four cardinal directions in an imaginary circle. At first I think they must be engaged in some sort of ritual dance for food, but then suddenly I know that they are calling something up from the depths of the ocean.

Just as I think I can stand the penetrating intensity of their call no longer, the once-still surface beneath them shatters. There is a burst of wings and water flying everywhere. Erupting from unnamed depths through the center of their circle, and hurling himself out of the water toward me, is an enormous alligator-man-god.

Ordinary consciousness is blown apart. It feels as if this being has exploded out of my cells. Drenched and terrified, I grab Beth protectively and leap to my feet, ready to run. In the split second before I act, I remember the earlier instruction: "Pay attention!" I take a long, deep breath to recover my composure as I search inwardly for the thread of meaning which might illuminate this startling event. As the fear ebbs away and the deep Earth-communion reasserts itself, I remember an earlier dream in the autumn in which I swam unharmed, and was in fact cherished and loved, among the alligators. I am reassured by the remem-bering of this and other similar dreams that I have nothing to fear from any of the Earth's native powers and creatures. This reptilian being, radiating such stunning, primal force, has been summoned here by the same purpose which has summoned me.

Further pieces of the night's work come rushing in. I sense that we are racing with time, getting all the alignments right before whatever is to happen can happen. Somehow I know there are still two remaining elements which must be activated.

The first becomes clear. On the other side of the sound, on the mainland I think, dancers are gathering in response to this night's summons. They are led by a deeply powerful woman—one whom the others look to for the healing, life-sustaining power she is able to call forth through the medium of the dance. Tonight, in preparation for what is to come, they will be dancing and drumming, opening power in the concentrated circles of ceremony.

Finally, Deborah appears before me—a shimmering, ethereal image. She speaks quickly and insistently, spurred on by the mounting pressure, saying that she and her husband, Ross, have been studying the movie, *E.T.* Somewhere in my mind, another voice picks up the sounds . . . I hear them whispered softly . . . "E . . . T . . . extraterrestrial . . . " Something fits—a key turning the tumblers of a lock . . . a door swinging open. . . . The ground underneath me gives way. The dream images start to slip, their coherence unravelling. I am sliding, spiraling downward with dizzying speed through an unlit passageway. The word "extraterrestrial" is whispered—thrumming, then rising into an avalanche of sound, ricocheting off the seemingly endless walls of this dark tunnel.

In a deafening roar, cells and consciousness cleave. Visions flash and whirl . . . the falling snow, the shrill calling of the birds, the alligator-god exploding out of the water, the pulsing drumbeat of the dance, the throbbing sounds . . . and then I am shot, rocket-like, away from Earth, out of body, out of time . . . into blinding, unspeakable light.

I waken into the unfolding of a vast story. At times a voice is speaking; at other times I am given a gestalt of images and sounds. Everything in me stretches to bring this story home:

There were beings of unimaginable breadth of consciousness and creativity, propelled from the heart and mind of God, who came to the newly-forming Earth to assist the divine impulse in creating the human race.

Certain aspects of divine awareness emanating from these beings were to be imprinted in the new race and within the physical body of the Earth. These awarenesses would then be triggered and released at specific synaptic "firing times," when new evolutionary patterns in human consciousness were to emerge. It was understood that in our present time, when the greatest of these expansions in consciousness would be undertaken, humanity would experience crises that were potent enough to destroy itself and life on Earth. In these most intense and critical periods, as humanity encountered its fears of destruction and the loss of so cherished a world, these imprints would leap the cellular gap, striking home like lightning, and firing their way into human awareness. In this great synthesis of consciousness and racial memory, these imprints would assist humanity in awakening to the divine dream within itself, within the Earth, within the universe.

These vast beings knew that knowledge of the sacred dimension — of all life's inherent divinity — would need to be rooted in the very soil and marrow of the Earth itself, so that humanity's encounters with the numinous, the divine, would be entwined with our encounters with the natural world, and would be everywhere mirrored in matter.

So they seeded the forming Earth's elements, encoding portions of themselves within matter — spirits of mountains . . . of wind . . . of trees . . . of creatures. They implanted essences which, when met with and penetrated by human love and consciousness, would reawaken humanity to our common origins and divine purpose. Beings of such stellar magnitude were not to remain within the planet's boundaries, however, for humanity's consciousness would have its own pathways to blaze and new continents of the mind to explore. They withdrew, merging consciousnesses into the bright star we call Vega. But always these divine imprints have lived and moved within the natural world, awaiting our recognition and reunion.

To ensure that the fundamental links with the sacred in nature were never lost, direct bonds containing this knowledge were established within the root peoples — the native, indigenous tribes of each continent. They became the guardians of the sacred Earth, though each race, and each person, would have its part to play in the overall development of the species. On our continent, the Native Americans have been the bearers of that wisdom.

I begin the return to waking consciousness, to my familiar bed — each cell stamped with unnameable light. I waken, feeling immersed in the power of the natural world and the medicines that the Indians have observed and worked with for many generations. These medicines are not some construct of a less sophisticated people, as the Native Americans have so often been portrayed in Western/white people's understanding, but are the seeds containing our deepest essence and purpose. They are the teachings given to us through the agency of our Creator and the divinely inspired, fully aware being which we call the Earth.

December 5, 1985

GATE OF THE GODDESS

Dreaming is startling. I waken into it to find myself stretched naked on what feels like an altar of stone . . . it is difficult to get this down on paper. My husband is standing guard near my head, and I can't see enough to discern where we are. This is so strange. I am thinking that, of course, this is my regular, flesh-and-blood body, but then I know it is more than that. I am fused with another body—is it of stone like the altar I lie on? Then an event occurs, and with it, I feel the disorientation lift . . . but not the startledness.

A woman dressed in a cleric's robe comes to the altar . . . she kneels on the stone prie-dieu. I am shocked to find her bending to kiss what I think is my navel. As she does this, the dream cracks open, and I am flooded with the image of a great stone Celtic cross. On it are the spirals of ancient Celtic knotwork used in the Book of Kells, and chiseled in the center of the cross is a primordial yonic image of the Goddess, named Bridget by the Celts. My heart starts to race wildly, for in some way I am inextricably bound within this stone cross of the Goddess. The clergy-woman reverently places her hands over the yoni at the center of the cross, and I feel, from within my placement inside the stone, a great release of power that flows out to her from this sacred vesica piscis. Then she stands, placing hands to her lips, and departs with head bowed in reverence, carrying the blessings of the Goddess with her on her journey.

January 30, 1986

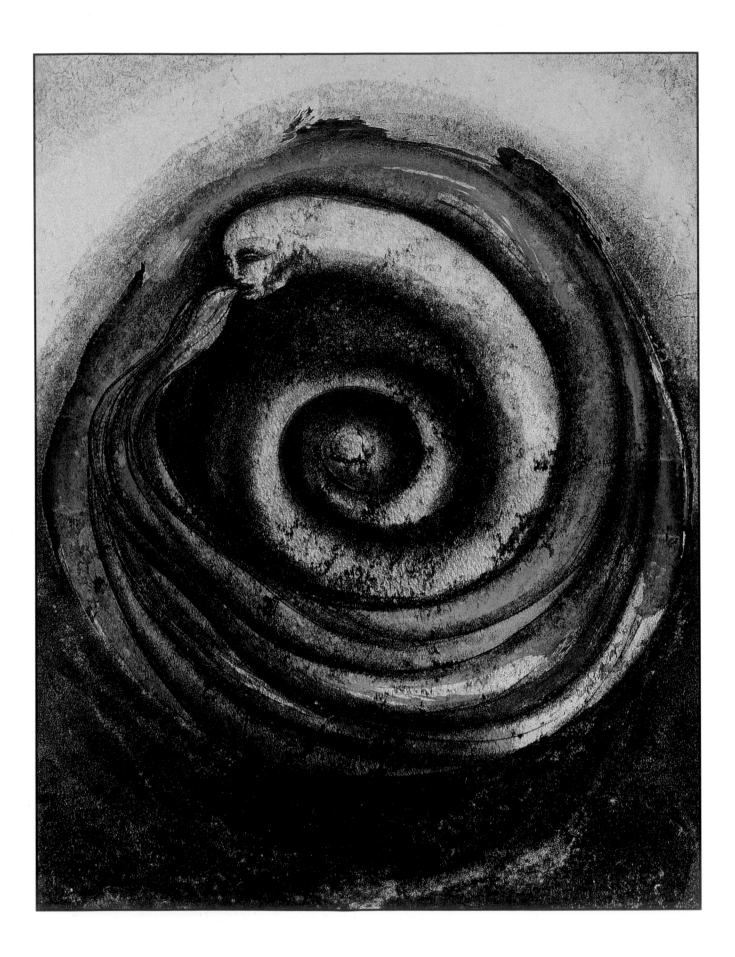

BIRTHSTONE

Throughout yesterday afternoon, an increasingly intense system of energy settles into my lower back. With it comes a sense of being drawn inward, and when nothing, not even my heating pad set on high, can match it, I remain in bed, listening for the inner coordinates that will unlock the message burning its way into my body . . .

Dreaming opens: There is no light, but I know from the smell and feel of the place that I am in a subterranean cave. I breathe deeply, filling my lungs with air so permeated with the substance and smell of rock and water that I can feel my body being fed, drinking in the elements in ways that living on the surface prevents. As I wait within the dark, I can feel my own energies begin to align with those of the dream. As they intersect, a reddish-brown stone wall emerges from the night of the cave, glowing with a soft light that seems to come from within the stone itself. I feel very detached but interested, when three circles are etched on the stone's face . . . It is then that I begin to understand that I am outside time as we know it, like in the recent *Sacred Island* dream. Here, there is only the stone, not seasonal changes, to tell me of the passing of the years — something the stones surely record, but in ways barely perceptible to ordinary human sight or awareness. I sense that I am watching the evolution of someone or something, over a millennium of time, and that these petroglyphs, emerging from the stone, are part of an ancient covenant made with the living Earth.

Then, imperceptibly at first, I become aware that the stone's vibration is changing . . . I begin to feel it in my body, right in my mid-section and lower back. I am startled into a heightened awareness as the three stone wheels somehow lift themselves out of the stone, spinning, and begin to move toward me. The center wheel expands, and I feel its spinning directly in my midsection. My mind begins to shape itself around a question of why, but the spinning becomes so powerful that all thought vanishes as I struggle just to maintain my focus in the cave. In the instant before the spinning disk reaches me, a flash of insight comes: this wheel is me. There are no explanations, just a rock-sure recognition. With that, the stone wheel's revolutions increase and it enters me, shattering my point of focus, sweeping away everything in the re-membering.

I waken, heart pounding, sheets and nightgown drenched with sweat. As I sit here to type out the night's work, I hear one phrase repeating itself over and over again. It is something the Cree medicine woman, Agnes Whistling Elk, said: "Birth was when the stones walked out of the Earth."[5]

February 4, 1986

SPIRIT OF THE MOUNTAIN

As we move through the evening routine with the children, I begin to feel harnessed by a deeper source of energy. For the remainder of the evening, until the kids are asleep, I feel like I'm moving in some sort of ritual pattern, aware that I am bringing everything into right relationship and harmony with this inner current. When I sit down to plan out the week's menus and grocery list, I sense that by doing this I have brought the family's life into focus too, since mealtimes are the sacramental gatherings of our day. There is a sweeping awareness that every single moment of our lives from birth to death is part of a great ceremony, a celebration, a liturgy of life. Our work is to waken to the mystery and wonder of it, to meet it consciously every day.

When the day's work is complete, I head off to bed, placing the quartz crystal I have recently begun to work with on my solar plexus. Several hours later I waken with a start. The crystal, carrying the memory of the planet, as all crystals do, has opened me to the full tide of that which I hear in the dream is called planetary evil. All through this segment of the night's work, I am penetrated by and experience the pain of scene after scene of energies which were too narrowly used by mankind: energies, actions, thoughtforms, and beliefs on the parts of individuals and civilizations which did not align in consciousness with the whole, but elevated only one people, or one system of thought, as being the whole of divine will—like Hitler and the development of the Third Reich and Aryan race supremacy. I am returned to my body and waking consciousness only long enough to anchor all of this, and then I am immediately plunged into further dreaming.

This time, I am aware of being surrounded by powerful beings of light. However, in and out of these luminous forms flicker various human beings of different races. Finally a form solidifies—a body to relate to my body. It seems to belong to someone of East Asian extraction.

It is then that I become aware that I am lying on some sort of operating table or hospital bed. There are others on similar beds, though I cannot see anything. Only my inner senses seem to have full operating capacity. Having had all the planetary events that marked separation from the Divine brought into our awareness and into the cellular substance of our bodies, these beings are now going to assist in purging this separation and in the healing the rift. As this process unfolds, all leaks in the circulatory system of Earth's energy field will be sealed as well. In response to our collective intent to work with and bond to the stones, and through our willingness to ground this quite literally, these beings of light have come to empower and assist us. I become aware that one of them is approaching my side with what I at first think is an enormous hypodermic syringe. As I feel one of these placed on either side of me, under my arms but angled in toward my solar plexus, I understand that these are crystals, and what I feel penetrating my body are not needles, but laser-like beams of light focused through the crystal tips. I feel a tremendous force flushing through me, and am startled as I realize that I have no skin to contain it. My body dissolves to become part of a vast primal sea of elemental energies. I am part of, but not separate from, the forces which coalesced in the formation of the Earth. As this takes place, I understand that all which has been out of balance in the planetary body is being transmuted by the anchoring and purging in my own and in other bodies. I hear a voice, as if from a great distance, saying that it will be three days before all will be cleared . . . and I hear the line from the Apostle's Creed, " . . . was crucified, dead and buried. He descended into hell. On the third day He rose again . . . "

Then the dream shifts. Those of us who have undergone the crystal cleansing have been gathered in San Francisco for an international expedition. In the next instant we are in some sort of flying vessel—not an ordinary plane. It changes shape many times during our flight, and is in such instant harmony with our needs that I determine that it is our collective consciousness which has constructed this vehicle. I am pleased to find that we are working together this cohesively already, and that although we have no idea of our destination, there is a deep trust that we will be taken where we need to go.

After some time, I feel our speed start to decrease, and as I look out the window, some jewel-like islands come shining into view. Without ever having been there, I know with great certainty that this is Japan, and the emanating force I feel, like the sun's rays but without the sun's warmth, is Fujiyama. At that moment, the mountain itself looms before me, breaking out of the mist that usually surrounds it. In response to an inner certainty, I announce to everyone: "This is why we are here! Open yourselves! *Let the mountain in!*"

Immediately we are admitted into the heart of the mountain and we hover near the ceiling of an inner cavern which is used as a temple or shrine. I laugh to myself, for we are now in single file, up in the air, trying to maneuver our vehicle to the ground. Since this is our first attempt, we haven't quite gotten all the procedures down properly, and about seven feet off the floor we lose our concentration and are dumped unceremoniously on the ground. We pull ourselves together and see our hosts, the people of the mountain, waiting quietly for us to introduce ourselves. One by one, everyone shares their names and their Earth lineages. As the sharing proceeds, I open to these people who have been awaiting our arrival.

I am most aware that everything they do is filled with meaning, and that every action is a studied, yet fluid work of art. Even the children are fully immersed in the way of the gods. I look down at my hands, then, and see that I am holding some sort of ceremonial bowl. With a gracious gesture, a young boy takes it from me and begins to make a paste by mashing together wild roots and herbs that have been grown and nourished by the spirit of the mountain. This is powerful medicine, made to be partaken of like the bread and wine of communion, and made to assist us in opening to the great mountain beings—not only Fujiyama, but others around the globe as well. I waken as I see the young boy sample the mixture and nod to everyone that it is ready and that the ceremony for which we have gathered is ready to begin.

Journal note: In checking *Earth Wisdom* several days later for some information on ceremony, I came across this sentence:

"Japan is the only modern nation which, due to fortuitous circumstances, has been able to carry its ancestral primitive relationship to the gods down to modern times as the root of its living culture."[6]

February 12, 1986

SPIRIT OF THE MOUNTAIN: PART II

When my dreaming opens, I feel as if I am peering into a very dark tunnel or cave—on the other end of which is the dream that waits for me this night. I travel to meet it, knowing I am moving very far away from my present body in both space and time. When the dream and I meet at last, this scene opens:

I am perched on the reddish-rock summit of a high desert mountain somewhere in what I think is the American Southwest. It is hot and dusty, but that is only a peripheral awareness. The main focus of my attention is the mountain under my hands. I run my hands over the stone, reaching into it, sensing into it, translating it as the blind translate Braille. Gradually, shapes emerge from within the mountain and carve themselves into the stone, so that they appear like petroglyphs. I am startled because I always thought that the stone markings were etched by people—yet here they have clearly been born from the rock itself. Something cracks open: inside, I feel veils parting, dissolving, and then my own speck of awareness swimming within this great being of stone, feeling its aliveness and a profound wisdom far exceeding my own. The mountain lets me know that any attempt to translate our encounter into language would be to give it expression through the lens of personhood. While there are times when that may be helpful in facilitating human understanding, what is to be done here requires that I release into the immensity of the mountain consciousness, into spirit-which-manifests-as-mountain, and let *it* translate and instruct me. I am stripped of words, my body consciousness disassembling to be reformed in a later time, bearing the imprints and knowledge of this ancient being.

When I am returned to the mountaintop, I see a friend there, wandering dazedly, holding onto the stone face for balance. Everywhere I look, the rock walls are carved with primitive animal figures. My friend has been so profoundly affected by some experience in this dream that she is unable to speak. She points first to one of the glyphs and then to herself. Not sure I understand, I ask her to repeat what she's signing to me in more detail. This time I understand. She says she didn't climb up here in the usual way, but that she emerged from within the rock and finally came out through the animal etching. I look around at all the other signs and leap to my feet, gasping with astonishment. Inside this mountain, inside these stone animal signs, is every member of our group! We look at each other, barely able to contain our excitement . . . as we have opened ourselves to the Earth and to the dream in the stones, we have been heard. She has taken us in.

The dream's focus narrows as two of these animal symbols, or animal medicines, are presented to me. The first is an alligator. I understand as I sit in its presence that this is Earth's seal of approval on the *Earthseeds* dream, and I am grateful for this affirmation. The second is a lion, and for the remainder of the night's work I enter the reality behind the sign and am instructed by this great cat. I am struck by the fact that this lion is larger than a horse, and in fact, preyed on wild horses. Repeated inner nudges remind me of descriptions of prehistoric cave lions. In a manner of teaching, it takes me inside—carrying me in its belly, giving me vision through its eyes. I am continually struck by its native grace and power, and by the harmony with which it lives in relationship to all other life—even in the manner in which it kills for food. After some time it shows me that, in this day and age, its teachings have largely been forgotten, and to those who would only study it objectively or scientifically, it would appear to be a decayed mass of bones and rotting flesh—evidence of its apparent failure to adapt. But as I watch a very graphic image of a decaying carcass being painted before me, out of the burial pit rises not a ghost of the lion but a newly resurrected creature, coat gleaming and muscles rippling with each supple movement. Again, for the second time in the dream, the awareness is brought home to me of that which our collective intent is opening: in our love for the Earth, and in our willingness to open to forms of consciousness other than human, we are tapping the power of, and beginning to open to, the purpose for which this abundant Earth and our habitation on it was called into being.

I am shown one last scene—what would appear to be a wilderness school or camp. Each of us in this class, and others who are waking to the dream of the sacredness of all life, are being trained here—city dwellers that we are—tapping the wilderness within, bonding with the Earth and meeting it within our own depths. I hear someone grumbling good-naturedly about how hard it is to stay this open, this aware of life. Another voice responds, "But that is the purpose of our disciplines! Chopping wood and carrying water keep us grounded and allow the teachings to have a place to root and grow in the soil of our everyday life."

The dream closes, and I waken to my four-year-old daughter tickling my feet.

March 4, 1986

GAIA

All I can bring back from this rather strange night of interrupted sleep is a powerful scene. I have stepped outside or through some doorway of consciousness. It is night, and as I look up into what I think is the night sky viewed from Earth, an enormous moon rises over the horizon. I remember the harvest moons from my childhood, because they always looked larger than the other moons of the year, but this moon is somehow different. I feel a thrill of excitement as I realize that this is not the moon, but that I am somewhere out in space looking back at our own planet. I feel my consciousness heighten and accelerate, and I wait to see what is to come. All over Earth there is a sense of a gathering presence, a brooding over the surface, and slowly a woman's face begins to shape itself out of the mists covering the planet. Up until this moment, I am only a witness to the emergence of this presence, but then knowing strikes, charging every cell.

"Gaia!" I gasp. The veils dissolve and I plummet, streaking earthward into the embrace of the oldest of divinities, the Earth Mother. I strike home, my body vibrating, fusing with hers, feeling her presence in every cell. I waken, wondering what this all means and why she has taken me in.

April 2, 1986

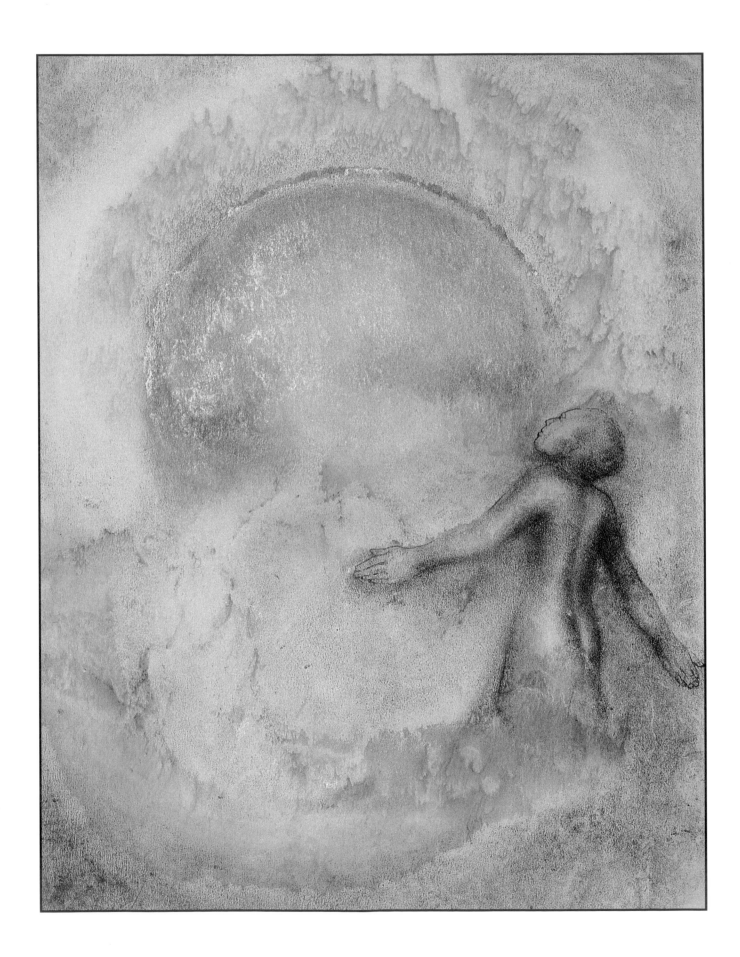

MESSAGES FROM THE DEEP

There has been much to the dreaming these days, but I am able to bring very little of it back over the threshold to waking. Of last night's work, one powerful scene remains:

At first I feel like I am peering through a dense fog. Gradually though, it begins to thin and clear as I focus all of my inner senses, and as the fog lifts I find I am sitting on the rocky ledge of a sweeping cove bordering the ocean. A small child is cradled in my arms—the same one I have been nurturing in other dreams for several weeks who is an archetypal synthesis of all races. I note that there are others who sit on this stony ledge with me, but so compelling is the dream's direction to look seaward that none of us turn our heads away from the water. As we watch, a great whale swims into the cove. My breath catches in my throat.

"Welcome!" I cry. As in other dreams, the lines of communication are open between the whale and me. It is so intent on its task that it does not reply directly to me, but instead I feel its mind moving within my own, shaping its thoughts into words. I hear the whale sensing into the emotional state of this gathering, knowing that interspecies communication requires certain alignments of the energy fields which we call emotions. With a kind of mischievous "Haruumph!" it tells me that what is to be communicated tonight can only be done in a spirit of joy.

Centering itself in our line of vision, it rises up out of the water and stares until everyone's attention has been gathered into a single focus. Then, with what feels like an impish grin, this great creature twists and dives, bringing its flukes down hard on the water and drenching us all with the salty spray. Everyone shrieks with delight, and the whale surfaces again, returning this time with two others. Shouts of glee fill the air as the three whales dive and splash, and the airborne water sparkles in the sun, setting the dream on fire with a million drops of light.

All across the ledge, people are leaping to their feet with abandon and diving into the ocean to swim with the whales. The whales respond with a lively welcome, caressing everyone with their flippers, bearing them on their broad backs, gently tossing them in the air—all accompanied by our laughter and astonished delight. I think to myself that, if not for this child I am caring for, I, too, would be out there swimming once again with my old friends. Immediately the whales speak into my mind:

"That you nourish this child is important—we will have other times to share these delights with you again. Your work tonight is as it is unfolding, for through you we may communicate this much needed message.

"Tell the children this: Tell the children there will be a world for them to grow up in.

"Tell the children this: Man is not the only species to determine the fate of the Earth."

When I return from the depths of this communion with the whales, there are tears running down my cheeks, for the current state of our world with the Libyan bombings has raised the ever-present threat of nuclear war before the world's eyes once again. For the first time, I can turn to the others on the ledge, knowing that I must tell them what the whales have said. Around the whole sweep of the curve sit, not adults as I somehow expected, but children from every nation in the world. As I gaze into each one's eyes, an intense maternal bond is instantly established between us. I move to each one, feeling their national identities as the bond is forged . . . Nicaragua . . . China . . . Denmark . . . Peru . . . America . . . and on around the globe until all have been named. I repeat the whales' message to them, filled as it is with the fullness of their and of all other species' love for the Earth and for our humanness.

I return slowly to my body, savoring the sweetness of the bond with the whales and with the children of the Earth, and feeling the sustaining hope that we will find our way through the years ahead.

April 21, 1986

THE SUNSTONE

Iwaken into dreaming traveling the now familiar wilderness landscape—that primal inner territory at the heart of all creation where self
is born from source. I am aware that my dreaming self knows the exact
location it has been called to, for I feel the magnetic pull that accompanies such travel. As I near the place of the night's work, I am excited,
wondering what is to come this new moon night.

When I reach my destination, I am far from any of the regions others
have explored and colonized in this inner territory. I look around,
flooded with remembering: I have been here before. I am standing in
front of a battered old cabin, its wood siding grayed and splintered, worn
by the passage of time and the work of the elements. I step up onto the
creaking porchboards, not sure whether they will hold my weight . . .
then I know that age has not weakened this place, but strengthened it.
Under my feet I can feel it growing out of the Earth, as rooted as a tree, as
solid as a mountain. Inside, in the first room of this two-room cabin, I
know I will find women in various stages of shamanic training. At one
time I, too, was one of these. Yet my work here now is to take me into
the second and innermost room of this place.

I cross the main room and approach the waiting door, collecting
myself as I step over the threshold. Inside there is a bed, a stack of crates
forming a rickety table, and an ancient grandmother whose body is as
weathered as the house itself and whose eyes are like smouldering coals
burning their way into my flesh. I feel my way along by a kind of inner
Braille, listening for how I am to move. The old woman doesn't speak,
and it is clear that, before she can or will, there is something I must do.

It is then that I see the heart-shaped stone lying in the middle of the
faded bedspread and I know what is required of me. I approach it, kneel
down, and place my hands on it, opening to a fusion of consciousness
with the stone. When molecular spin of body and stone reach the same

velocity, the stone begins pulsing like a heart and radiating a warm glow. In the same second, my own body lights up. Instantly, I know that the purpose of this fusion is to make sure my physical body has the stamina to carry the work ahead. The old woman and I read my auric field. All is clear, in balance, fertile. I rise, carrying the stone with me. I lay it carefully in front of her, and as she rests her hands upon the still-glowing stone, she begins to speak:

"This stone to which you have attuned yourself does not have its origins on the Earth. It is a sunstone, originating in the heart and mind of the solar logos. As such, it carries concentrated solar energies meant to be released on the Earth through the ancient priesthood of Melchizedek, also called the Priesthood of the Sun, in which you have long known your involvement . . . "

As she pauses, I say, "All my life I have carried a special stone in my pouch which I call my sunstone . . . " I reach inside the soft leather bag and pull out the stone. It reminds me of the inside of a geode, yet this is like a crystal ball composed of many crystal clusters growing out of some central core. It is fiery red and flashes blindingly as I hand it to her.

"Yes," she says slowly, drawing information out of the stone, "This too, is a sunstone. But what we are talking about here concerns orders of magnitude. The stone you have carried has been your transmitting link within this ancient order. What this new stone represents is an energy base more concentrated than any yet sustained on the planet. With the fusion of its energies with you and others in the priesthood who are currently in incarnation, a new field of resonance will be set in motion on the Earth."

"Then I am to be a bearer of this new stone?" I ask.

"Yes," she replies, "but not just yet. To bring it in fully right now would be more than the planet could sustain. We will need a year of initiatory gestalts of increasing intensity to prepare the way. All your awarenesses and the state of the culture around you will reflect the disruption of those patterns which no longer serve the deepest purposes for which the Earth was called into being. Think of this as a clearing of the way. There are new impulses of creation for all the Earth, and deep spiritual wakenings for humanity, which will come through the union with the stone. When all is ready, the stone will be given."

I ride her last words back to waking, still remembering the shape and the aliveness of the sunstone under my hands.

May 8, 1986

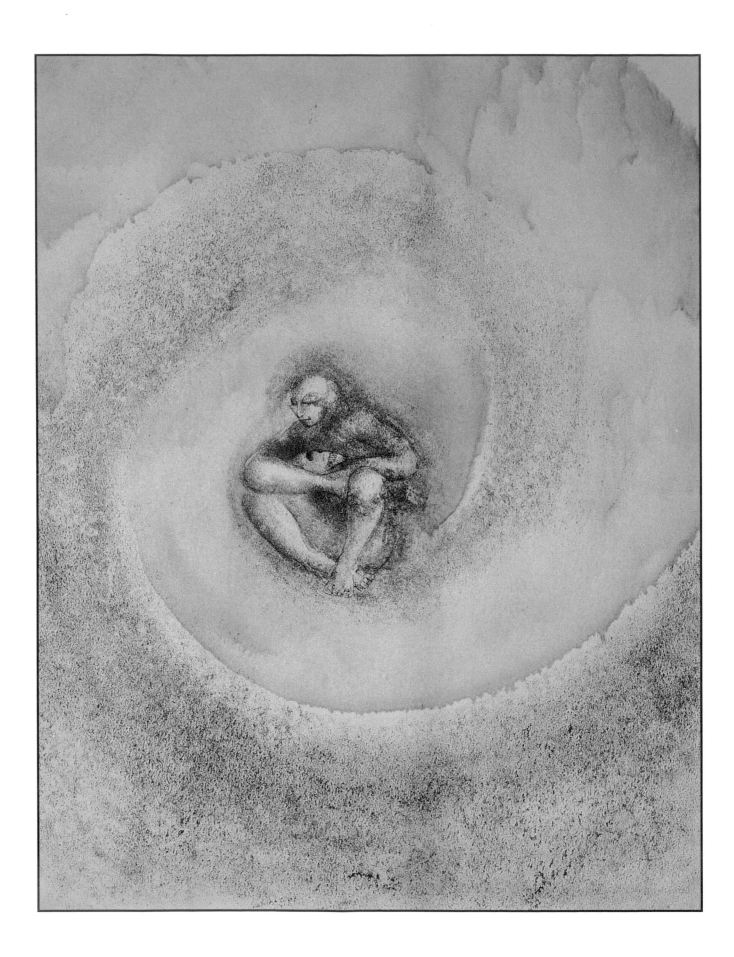

FIRST MOTHER

As I start tracking the dreaming, I am aware that it feels complex and involved. My first response is to look for signs or landmarks which will tell me where I am. This is not familiar territory and, as in other such dreams over the years, I know that I have been set down in an inner landscape which is not my own. I am intrigued, loving the high adventure that always accompanies such times.

I am in a huge hall, in the midst of what, at first, appears to be some sort of celebration for a woman I don't know. She, and the women friends who have put on the party for her, are all in their mid-fifties to mid-seventies. They are all dressed in expensive, well-tailored, casual clothes. As I stand in the midst of the dream, I am pushing at the edges of awareness, wondering: Why here? Why these women?

As if in response to my question, the lamp table from our den materializes. The table is minus the lamp, however, and holds only the two pictures of my grandmothers I have always displayed there. I have an odd sense, then, that these women have been waiting for me to arrive with these pictures, and that, strangely, it is I who am the guest of honor. I look up from where the table has just appeared to find them circled around me. They eagerly ply me with questions about my grandmothers. Story-lover that I am, I am delighted to be able to evoke my family's matriarchal roots, sharing Mabel Grace and Effie Rose with these women, who, for some unnamed reason, appear to be keenly interested in my family history. On impulse, I decide that I will take the photographs out of their frames, for I sense that handling the pictures will bring my grandmothers' lives into greater immediacy for us all. As I slip the backs of the frames out of their grooves, I discover that, unknown to me, another photograph has been sandwiched between the old photos and the cardboard backing. Before I even turn it over, I know it is a picture which will hold great personal meaning for me. I assume it must be a likeness of my great grandmother who died before I was born, and about whom I was told many stories. My next thought is that Aunt June must have inadvertently tucked it away here many years ago and forgotten it. I am thrilled to find this unexpected treasure, and the women lean over my hands, as excited as I am about rediscovering this part of my heritage. I gingerly turn it over, for it is yellowed and brittle, aware that this will be the first time this woman's presence will have been seen for many years.

I am spun into a state of confusion, shaking my head in an attempt to clear my vision. The photograph begins to blur, losing its shape before our eyes; the molecules composing it visibly disassemble to form a new image. The woman in turn-of-the-century dress disintegrates, and out of the disappearing image of my great-grandmother emerges an ancient ceremonial dancer standing on a windy desert plain or mesa.

Her head is bent down toward the Earth, but when the scene has fully assembled, she slowly and deliberately lifts her head and raises her arms to me, reaching out beyond the flat two-dimensionality of the picture. I feel the concentrated power of her motion in my middle, nearly vomiting with its impact. In a powerful rush, I am pulled headlong into the scene, into the midst of what something in me calls the "Corn Dance." Hair-raising impulses pound up my spine, and every cell in my body is charged with a supernormal consciousness. I am only peripherally aware that I work to steady myself with carefully drawn breaths.

My attention is riveted on the figure before me. She is a Native American elder—a grandmother. But what nearly hurls me out of the dream is the mask she wears. She is so at one with this archetype that the mask seems to have become part of her skin. She *is* the crone, she *is* the Corn Mother come to life in this most ancient of ceremonies.

Dried husks of corn are bound about her. It seems, then, that all I hear is the rustling of dried corn stalks in the wind. I know there are other dancers—all elders, all medicine women—somewhere in the background, but I cannot tear my eyes away from the mask. It is the eyes, I think to myself, the eyes of this strangely compelling mask which draw me in . . .

The ground drops dizzyingly away. I find myself no longer staring into the eyes of the mask, but into the cavernous eyes of an ancient skull which I know, though it defies ordinary reason, is alive.

My falling continues, out of body, out of perceivable form. I am swept into a flood of images, feeling myself part of a force beyond any description . . . primal, infinite, yet exquisitely and intimately cherishing—

the Power by which we all are named, the author of life. I am submerged in this great tide, feeling it creating the unifying field of the physical world. This source—this creative, luminous, most *glorious* essence—is the "God stuff" present within the cells of every living thing, and of every human being ever to walk the Earth.

Deep surging waves carry me. I know without seeing that I am within the skull, carried there by the impulses of this unnameable Creator—bone-former, life-maker. This skull is the origin, the model, the prototype, the first casing for the complex species which will allow Earth to waken, to think and reflect upon herself . . . the structure which will give rise to *consciousness becoming conscious of itself*—a consciousness able to knowingly link with its creative source and recognize its divine birth.

The tide throbs and swells like a vast, pulsing heart, and I am carried back to my dream body, now cradling the skull in my hands. Yet part of me remains within the depths of the dream, permeated by the deep primordial memory of this skull that I call the First Mother—womb of the human race, cradle of civilization. She lives within me: a slow burning ember of consciousness . . . bone within my bone, flesh within my flesh.

As the dream closes, I am trying to reorient myself in the hall, making fumbling attempts to find the pictures of Effie and Mabel which somehow disappeared under the impact of the Grandmother's appearance. I dazedly sift through the objects and papers still on the table, knowing all the while that the dream's power has burned through everything and that I will not find the photos again.

November 13, 1986

THE ROCK

During the years in which Deborah has been touch-drawing and I have been charting dream territory, there has been much for us to absorb. The learning has been rich and deep, nourishing, at times surprising, and always empowering. What remains a personal constant and is, for us, the foundation and context through which the dreams and drawings emerge, is perhaps best described in these two final dreams:

August 21, 1986

In this dream, I am with a large gathering of people at what appears to be an ocean. This ocean, however, unlike the bodies of water we are familiar with, is at the "edge" of the Earth—an intersection of consciousness where the creative impulses that guide and inform all life merge with the environment in which we live out the dramas of our daily lives. We stand near the water's edge, watching immense and seemingly interstellar waves crashing on the shore. I am conducting a seminar on how to be in right relationship with the energies bearing down on our planet.

A certain distance out from the shore is a great, craggy mountain of stone rising from the depths of this boundless primal ocean—a rock which grows out of the creative source of life as we know it. I divide the assembly into small groups and then guide everyone out to this place in the short intervals between the waves. When at last we are all gathered on the rock, I speak about the stone as everyone imprints it, holding fast to it in the buffeting of wind and spraying of sea.

"This rock is the foundation on which our lives are anchored," I say.

"In these turbulent times of the changeover from one pattern of consciousness to the next, it is to these roots of stone you must hold. Here you will find the peace and serenity that surpasses understanding. When your living honors the source of your being and the source of all creation —for they are one and the same—the waves that wash away old forms will do their work, and you, who find your transcendent identity apart from form, will not grieve this passing. Form, and relationships based on form, build up and die down. There is always 'a time for every purpose under heaven.' Yet that which sustains and creates all form—the living presence of God—is never destroyed, never dies. Trust in the divine plan for all our lives and for this green Earth, and though you may shed some tears at the passing of forms which now fall away, do not be dismayed. The love that gave them birth now reaches beyond them to create a fuller expression. 'Behold!' It says. 'I make all things new!'

"Trust in the path unfolding before you. It will always create its own way and will give rise to whatever forms will be appropriate to your ministries. All you are asked is to hold to your knowing of the roots and the source, and these, in turn, will carry you through the most turbulent times unscathed, yet not unchanged.

"Now, from the roots, you must listen! There will be a wave that calls your name, and when this comes you must catch it and ride it to the shore. From it, you will receive knowledge of the next steps you are to take. In any case—whether you are riding the waves or planting your feet on the shores of the awakening land—do not forget the rock. It is the foundation of all you are, and it will never forsake you."

September 3, 1980

THE OUTPOURING

Imove into sleep, feeling myself traveling far away from my body— at once a voyage out beyond the limits of our solar system, as well as into the innermost constellation of my own identity. There is a moment when I feel the necessary alignments for the night's work moving into place . . .

Everything cracks open, born out of indescribable light. And then a voice is thundering through me, edged with fire. It is transmitted over measureless distances, finally coming home to our planet as massive lightning bolts striking their destination. The message crackling through the atmosphere is for the peoples of the Earth:

"Witness the lightning! Feel its imprints within you, for now the flood waters approach! All that has been prepared for these many years is imminent, and comes with all the strength and power of the mighty waters of Aquarius which will pour out over the Earth. Throughout the land, you hear the distant rumble of waters grown so full and heavy that they will burst through the dams of human making and sweep all limitations away. This is the outpouring which will carry us on its crest. This is the time when all humanity must lift up the light together, and in doing so, transform the Earth.

"Do not fear the onrushing waters. I repeat: *there is nothing to fear!* You who work for the rising of the light within the human race must know that the outpouring itself has been invoked by all humanity. Yet few truly comprehend the power of their prayers for peace. These forces are of such magnitude that, had not all of humanity invoked them, they would sweep you away.

"Yet through this race's evolution, all who shepherd the Earth have nurtured the emerging human consciousness through its evolutionary process. No energies are released to the Earth that are not invoked by humanity itself. Truly the prayers must be lifted up by the multitudes before the energies of planetary initiation are opened. These energies that approach the Earth are the most powerful yet, for they bring you to the birth of a new planetary consciousness. The labor pains of this emerging awareness sweep the planet now, for this birth comes from humanity's own heart, as it always must.

"Do not question the hows, the outworkings, nor where all this will lead you, for these mental wanderings divert you from the present, the point of power, and create limited channels for manifestation. Instead, release your most cherished judgments, and ride these waters with your spiritual disciplines and deepest communions. Strive to embrace the Earth, to embrace the most ordinary, insignificant-seeming rhythms of your daily life with an unlimited, unconditional love, for all things are made holy through love.

"These times require the highest of visions. Only in the most elevated reaches of your attuning will you be able to move gracefully with the outpouring. If any part of you is attached to any form or any relationship that separates you from your own timeless divine essence, you will experience the force of these waters bursting through the barriers of your belief. These initiatory energies will shake you to the very core, and will demand the release of all such ties, even to that which you have loved and held so dearly. How many of you have cried, 'Oh no! Not that too!,' and how often have you been stripped to stand naked in God's light?

"There can be no barriers. All initiation involves releasing identification with an aspect of self/divinity you have known. All who know the power of initiation are aware of that moment of blindness and of the leap of faith that is made when all shreds of what has been known are released, and the 'yes' is given, even in the face of fears which murmur that this is all a fantasy of fools, and that you have given up all for naught.

"Yet I say to you, all who have opened to these outpourings in other times know that, in such leaping, all is given and all is transformed. So do not resist the releasing. Do not hold on, but let the waters flow through, cleansing and clearing. Though you may at times feel you will be swallowed up and drowned by the flood's power, know this will not be so, and that again there is nothing to fear. What will be shaken free from its moorings is the timeless essence that has encased itself in matter, for divinity cannot be contained in form. When humankind truly knows this, you will see how it can be expressed and reflected *through* form, and then truly will the City of Light emerge on this planet.

"In the times ahead, all humanity will experience the rending of a veil that has both protected and blinded. You who are able must release yourselves to the dynamic resting places of the Most High. Here, you will blaze like beacon fires, illuminating the path ahead, flames of the One Light.

"There is no turning back. Yet who of you knew the full implications of what it meant to cry for wholeness? To know Truth? And yet all of you knew it was unalterably your true path, and you chose it willingly and surely, however blindly. So it is for humanity now, and those of you who can must sing the song of peace, and light the way home."

September 20, 1979

AFTERWORD

What we have shared in these pages are the fruits of years of inner exploration. Dreams and touch-drawing are two of the many pathways which integrate the inner and outer realms. If you are drawn to working with your dreams, there are many resources and perspectives available to support your exploration, including many excellent dream dictionaries. Yet, in contrast, with all the volumes on art, there is little written on how to enter the realm of inner imagery.

Touch-drawing makes the doorway to this realm particularly accessible, even to the most inexperienced artist. The process eliminates the need for tools, allowing impressions to well up directly from the subconscious, through the fingertips and onto paper which has been laid on a freshly painted surface. It is a form of artistic meditation—simple, direct, yet drawing from great depths.

With a few basic materials and instructions, it is possible to open that door and begin a journey of creation. In this spirit, we offer the process of touch-drawing.

MATERIALS AND SET UP

- Tube of oil paint or lithography ink (with children, use a water-base block printing ink)
- Soft rubber printing roller (available at most art supply stores)
- A piece of glass, plastic or any smooth, non-absorbent surface
- Enough lightweight paper to allow you to draw freely: freezer or butcher paper, onionskin, bond, tissue paper, newsprint, sumi, even surgical table paper works.
- Experiment!

TECHNIQUE

Touch drawing requires no special space to set up. A drawing board can be stored behind furniture and slipped out at any time. You may place the board flat on a table, or lean the top of the board on a table with the bottom set in your lap. Whether you use a low table or not, you can sit in a meditation position on the floor. It is advisable to wear old clothes or a smock.

Squeeze a small amount of paint from the tube onto the glass, and spread it over the surface with the roller. Now place a sheet of paper on top of the paint. Close your eyes and begin drawing by moving your hands, (try both at once!), and fingertips and nails around the paper. Don't worry at first about "making a picture." When one sheet feels complete, pull it off the glass and put on a new sheet of paper and try again.

Allow a series of images to evolve, without worrying about each one being "perfect."

Experiment with eyes open and closed, one hand and two.

If a sense of imagery naturally begins to emerge, go with it. Or you may wish to continue working with the abstract flow of energy, as if you are giving a massage. What's important is that you be yourself!

When you feel complete, go back to the first drawing and look at the whole series. See the drawings as traces of a living process—you may be surprised by their beauty, mystery or honesty.

There is no need to clean the glass and roller after working—just let them dry and use again.

SOME THOUGHTS ON BRINGING THE PROCESS INTO YOUR LIFE

Touch Drawing is very mobile. You can bring materials with you to a workshop, concert, friend's house, or into the natural environment. If you work outside, bring a couple of clips to keep the paper from blowing off the board and something to hold down your pile of paper.

You may also like to add color to your drawings with pastel, colored pencil, or watercolor, or try using several drawing boards, each rolled with a different color. The variations on the process are infinitely open to your exploration.

You may like to set up a regular time to draw, as you might for meditation. A magical time is when you have just awakened and are still half in dreams. The depth of the night is a sacred time when the outer world falls away. Just remember that you don't have to make a production of sitting down to draw. So much can happen with even a half hour of working.

See it as a journey, an exploration. Acknowledge yourself in the moment, project this state of being out onto the page, and reflect upon it briefly. The very act of releasing this image will put you into a new state of being, which you may again pour through your fingertips and onto the page. Do your best not to pass judgment on each drawing as it comes through; each is just a stepping stone to the next. As you gaze into the inner mirror of Touch Drawing you may find yourself transforming literally before your own eyes.

If you care to continue and deepen the process, do not allow yourself to be stopped by your dissatisfaction with what you are doing. Sometimes it may be uncomfortable, even painful, to continue drawing, but think of this as the pangs of birth—you are birthing your soul! Later, when you look through the tracings of your journey, you may find there is much more than you could appreciate in the moment you created it. Many of the drawings I now hold most dear I thought nothing of when they first emerged.

Having a companion share the process is wonderful—whether they draw with you or simply witness your drawings. If you have a particularly enigmatic image, it can be helpful to reflect upon it through writing. It is good to number and date a series after it has been done. This way the drawings can work as a visual journal. Looking at an old drawing is like being given the memory of a dream from long ago.

What I have shared here is merely a starting point. Feel free to go where your own path leads you. Take the process into yourself, and let your Self pour through!

1. Dolores LaChapelle, *Earth Wisdom* (Los Angeles: The Guild of Tutors Press 1978), p. 23.
2. Barbara G. Walker, *The Women's Encyclopedia of Myths and Secrets* (San Francisco: Harper and Row, 1983), p. 523.
3. Tony Shearer, *Lord of the Dawn, Quetzalcoatl* (Happy Camp: Naturegraph Publishers, 1971).
4. Dolores LaChapelle, *Earth Festivals* (Silverton: Finn Hill Arts, 1973), pp. 7-8.
5. Lynn V. Andrews, *Flight of the Seventh Moon: The Teaching of the Shields* (San Francisco: Harper and Row, 1984), p. 55.
6. LaChapelle, *Earth Wisdom*, p. 86.

About the author:

Marcia S. Lauck, is founding director of Four Circles Foundation (1977-), a contemplative community in San Jose, California. Her work is guided by the heartfelt belief that the foundations of lasting global peace and a profound renewal of the human spirit lie within us and must be nurtured by each human being. In addition to serving as director of the community, she maintains a private counseling practice. She has presented a variety of in-depth workshops on dreams which weave together the waking-dreaming connection, creation-centered spirituality, community-building through dreamwork, and the sacred earth traditions. She is an avid skater, guitarist and vocalist. Marcia, her husband, and their two daughters reside in a 1906 home which they have restored.

About the artist:

Deborah Koff-Chapin, (B.F.A. Cooper Union) has been developing the process of Touch Drawing since it was revealed to her through ecstatic play in 1974. Her drawings have been exhibited nationally, and have been published in *The Womanspirit Sourcebook* (Harper & Row, 1988), *Dromenon Journal, Parabola, In Context* and *Woman of Power*. Deborah has been sharing the process of Touch Drawing at conferences, workshops and ceremonials around the United States and Canada for many years. She is also a certified expressive therapist (A.E.T.A.) and an improvisational vocalist. It is her deeply held belief that the artist's role in our time is to revitalize the sacred function of the arts, and to help consecrate and give form to the emergence of a new culture. Deborah resides with her husband and daughter in Whidbey Island, Washington, where she teaches periodically through the Chinook Learning Center. If you would like more information on her art work, please send a stamped, self-addressed envelope (2 oz. postage), plus $3.00 to her via Bear & Co., P.O. Drawer 2860, Santa Fe, NM 87504-2860